ORWELL

1984

NOTES

COLES EDITORIAL BOARD

Bound to stay open

Publisher's Note

Otabind (Ota-bind). This book has been bound using the patented Otabind process. You can open this book at any page, gently run your finger down the spine, and the pages will lie flat.

ABOUT COLES NOTES

COLES NOTES have been an indispensible aid to students on five continents since 1948.

COLES NOTES are available for a wide range of individual literary works. Clear, concise explanations and insights are provided along with interesting interpretations and evaluations.

Proper use of COLES NOTES will allow the student to pay greater attention to lectures and spend less time taking notes. This will result in a broader understanding of the work being studied and will free the student for increased participation in discussions.

COLES NOTES are an invaluable aid for review and exam preparation as well as an invitation to explore different interpretive paths.

COLES NOTES are written by experts in their fields. It should be noted that any literary judgement expressed herein is just that — the judgement of one school of thought. Interpretations that diverge from, or totally disagree with any criticism may be equally valid.

COLES NOTES are designed to supplement the text and are not intended as a substitute for reading the text itself. Use of the NOTES will serve not only to clarify the work being studied, but should enhance the reader's enjoyment of the topic.

1984, by George Orwell.
First published in Great Britain in 1949
by Martin Secker & Warburg Limited
©1949 Estate of Eric Blair

ISBN 0-7740-3326-6

© COPYRIGHT 1989 AND PUBLISHED BY
COLES PUBLISHING COMPANY
TORONTO—CANADA
PRINTED IN CANADA

Manufactured by Webcom Limited
Cover finish: Webcom's Exclusive **Duracoat**

CONTENTS

Page No.

George Orwell: Life and Works

George Orwell, whose real name was Eric Blair, was born in 1903, in Bengal, India, the son of a minor official in the Indian Civil Service. As was customary, his mother brought him, along with his two sisters, back to England when he was eight to be educated.

Orwell was sent to a boarding school on the south coast, a school whose students were largely sons of the wealthy. To attract such students, the school concentrated mainly on "cramming" boys for entrance to Harrow and Eton. Orwell was one of a few bright boys allowed to attend at a lower tuition, a practice followed to ensure the winning of scholarships for the honor of the school. He came from what he himself called the "lower-upper-middle class" and hence was subjected to the snobbery of the other boys and the headmaster and his wife. He would later write that the psychological pressure set his mind for life and, although many critics now feel that he tended to adopt poses in his autobiographical writing, the situation must have been oppressive for a sensitive child.

Orwell went to Eton in 1917 on a scholarship. The atmosphere was freer there, he made friends and he read a good deal. He also encountered, for the first time, popular liberal and socialist ideas. Such ideas were common subjects of discussion at Eton, especially in this period immediately following World War I. When he graduated in 1921, he decided not to go on to a university, though he could have. Instead, he joined the civil service and went to Burma as a sergeant in the Indian Imperial Police.

Orwell served in Burma from 1922 to 1927. As a policeman, he was, of course, the embodiment of British imperialism to the natives, a painful reversal of roles in comparison to his life as a schoolboy. He intensely disliked being the instrument by which power was exercised over the Burmese; on the other hand, he had to play the part of one in authority. When he returned to England on leave in 1927, he resigned his post.

For various reasons, not all of them clear even to Orwell himself, he then deliberately chose to live among poor working people in Paris and among tramps in England for more than a year. These experiences formed the basis for his first book, an autobiographical work he called *Down and Out in Paris and*

London, published in 1933. Although he had published some early writing under his real name, the first book used the name "George Orwell." He later explained that he took the last name from an English river near which he had once lived and the first as typically English. In any case, it was probably a symbolic act signalling his choice of vocation as well as his attitude toward his own country.

During these years, he worked as a teacher and, after he married, he and his wife kept a village tavern and general store. His income was small, and his first book brought him very little success. His first novel, *Burmese Days*, based on his experiences in Burma, came out in 1934. In 1935, he published another novel, *A Clergyman's Daughter*, which makes use, in part, of his teaching experience.

Although by now he had received critical comment in a few places, he was not making enough income from his writing to depend on it entirely. The novel, *Keep the Aspidistra Flying*, published in 1936, was based on his experiences at this time as a clerk in a bookstore. He became an active socialist during this period and, when his publisher encouraged him to visit a depressed industrial area and write about his personal reactions, he took the opportunity to put his political convictions into action. The results of his trip, *The Road to Wigan Pier*, came out in 1937.

Meanwhile, the Spanish Civil War had broken out and, though Orwell went as an observer and reporter, he soon enlisted on the Republican side. By chance, he joined a militia loyal to the P.O.U.M. (*Partido Obrero de Unificación Marxista*; the Workers' Party of Marxist Unification), a Marxist but anti-Stalinist political party, rather than the better known (at least in America at the time) International Brigade, which was ultimately communist-controlled. He was badly wounded on the front and, by the time he recovered from the wound, the Republican government was dominated by communist groups responsive to direction from Russia, and the purge of other political parties, including the P.O.U.M., was under way. Orwell and his wife were forced to leave Spain for fear of imprisonment and possible summary execution. What he saw in Spain shocked him badly. He believed the communists' actions there had betrayed a popular revolution that might otherwise have given the working classes true freedom and status. The book he wrote from his Civil War experience, *Homage to Catalonia*, published in 1938, reflected this idea of the revolution betrayed, an idea that would find its ultimate form in *Animal Farm*.

Upon his return to England, Orwell published another novel, *Coming Up for Air*, in 1939. This was the first of his books to sell at all well. The war, which he had predicted in this book, was soon under way and, although he tried to enter the army, he was rejected for service because of the tuberculosis from which he suffered all his life. He was accepted in the Home Guard, however, and, during World War II, he also worked for a time in the Indian Service of the British Broadcasting Corporation.

Two collections of essays, *Inside the Whale, and Other Essays* and *The Lion and the Unicorn: Socialism and the English Genius*, appeared in 1940 and 1941. In addition, during this time, Orwell did a great deal of political journalism. A regular column, "As I Please," appeared in the *London Tribune*; and he contributed to *The Observer, Manchester Evening News, Partisan Review* and *New Leader*.

In 1945, Orwell published the first of the two books for which he is generally known, *Animal Farm*. An anti-utopian novel, like *1984*, it is cast in the form of an animal satire. The obvious subject of the satire is Soviet Russia, but more generally it has to do with totalitarianism of any kind. The success of the book in Great Britain and the United States gave Orwell an income he had never before enjoyed.

Dickens, Dali, and Others, another collection of essays, appeared in 1946. With the death of his wife in the same year, Orwell had the complete care of his adopted son. In order to find the time to complete a book which embodied the ideas that concerned him most at this time, he moved to the Scottish Hebrides. His most celebrated book, *1984*, was published in 1949. In it, Orwell presents a near-future society that is an ominous projection of totalitarianism in the contemporary world. Although he remarried and was planning new work for the future, he died in London, in early 1950, from poor health and exhaustion.

Two other collections of essays appeared shortly after his death: *Shooting an Elephant, and Other Essays*, in 1950, and *Such, Such Were the Joys*, in 1953.

3

Orwell's Major Works

1933. *Down and Out in Paris and London* (autobiography).
1934. *Burmese Days* (novel).
1935. *A Clergyman's Daughter* (novel).
1936. *Keep the Aspidistra Flying* (novel).
1937. *The Road to Wigan Pier: On Industrial England and its Political Future* (sociology).
1938. *Homage to Catalonia* (history).
1939. *Coming Up for Air* (novel).
1940. *Inside the Whale* (essays).
1941. *The Lion and the Unicorn: Socialism and the English Genius* (pamphlet).
1945. *Animal Farm* (satire).
1946. *James Burnham and the Managerial Revolution* (pamphlet).
Critical Essays (essays).
1949. *1984* (novel).
1950. *Shooting an Elephant* (essays) published posthumously.
1953 *Such, Such Were the Joys* (autobiography) published posthumously.
1968. *Collected Essays, Journalism and Letters* (4 volumes) published posthumously.

Orwell, Communism and Socialism

It is impossible to appreciate Orwell's work fully without understanding his political views, yet, in North America especially, students often misunderstand them. Many are surprised to learn that, although he was an outspoken anti-communist, he was also an ardent socialist all his life.

The failure to distinguish between socialism and communism causes the confusion. Socialism refers generally to any economic system based on the ownership of goods and property, collectively (by all or a large part of society) rather than by individuals. The idea was described at least as early as Plato's *Republic* (fourth century B. C.) and was practised by the early Christians. In its modern forms, those developed since the 1830s, socialism preaches government ownership of goods and control of their production and distribution. It does not usually insist on the abolition of private property, though it seeks to regulate this insofar as it affects public interests. Many variations of socialist beliefs and practice exist.

Communism is a specific form of socialism, developed from principles laid down by Karl Marx and Friedrich Engels in the *Communist Manifesto* (1847) and *Das Kapital* (1867-94). Although recent decades have seen some variations arise in its methods and politics, it always seeks the abolition of private property. And it advocates, at least in theory, the wresting of ownership, production and control of goods by violent revolution. Socialists, on the other hand, seek to obtain the means of production by legal and relatively peaceful means.

Socialism has a long and respected tradition in Great Britain and many parts of Europe, where it has attracted the allegiance of many thinkers and artists, as well as politicians, for well over a century. In mild forms, it is often the policy of legitimate political parties and democratically elected governments.

Since about the 1890s, many of Great Britain's intelligentsia have been socialists; indeed, during the 1920s through the 1940s socialism was almost the norm in many artistic circles. Surely, they thought, there must be a better way of organizing a world that was suffering the aftermath of World War I, growing industrialization, the great Depression (and several smaller, earlier ones), the rise of fascism and the bitter Spanish Civil War. There

5

was much disagreement about specifics, however, and great theoretical battles were waged among the literary adherents of various schools of thought.

One problem for these Western socialists was how to react to communism as it was evolving in Soviet Russia after the Revolution of 1917. It was, at that time, the only government in the world based on completely socialistic principles, and many socialists elsewhere felt they had to give it some support, even if they disagreed with part of its theoretical basis. As history unfolded, Soviet propaganda, secrecy and isolation made it difficult for others even to know what was going on in Russia. Rumors drifted out, but they were just that — rumors. It is difficult for us to realize today that until the 1950s the world did not know the truth about the outrages committed by Stalin or the shape communism had taken. And, when the Soviet Union entered World War II on the Allied side, many people thought that it might be better not to know, or that communism's opposition to fascism was so important as to be worth ignoring other aspects of the theory and its practice.

Orwell disagreed, as he showed in writing *Animal Farm* and then *1984*. But, he had been disagreeing with many other socialists for much of his adult life. Even before he wrote these books, much of his writing, especially his essays and newspaper articles, had involved criticism of socialism as well as advocacy of it.

Early on, he had insisted that it was necessary for socialism to separate itself from utopian idealism, arguing that although socialism was the only hope of the world, it could not claim to make society perfect. He had also directed much criticism at the socialist British Labour Party, claiming that it preached not genuine socialism, which should be concerned with the welfare of all people, but only the advancement of members of British labor unions. In addition, he advocated the setting up of a United States of Europe, which, he said, by including about half the skilled workers of the then-industrialized world under a socialist government, would spread socialist policies throughout the rest of the world by example.

Orwell's anti-communism also appeared early. During the 1930s, he admitted only suspicions, pointing out how difficult it was to discover the truth about what was going on in Soviet Russia. For example, he pointed out that evidence and statistics suggested its people were simultaneously the hungriest and the best fed, the most advanced and the most backward, the happiest and the most miserable people in the world. By 1941, however, when many others were praising the cleverness of Stalin's foreign policy in its wavering between alliance and enmity toward Germany, he said the policy would eventually be recognized as opportunistic and stupid. When *Animal Farm* appeared in 1945 (it was written in 1943), Orwell had no intention of deceiving anyone with its allegory. And, by 1948, he wrote openly, in *The Observer*, of the communist experiment as a lost revolution:

> Placed as they were, the Russian Communists necessarily developed into a permanent ruling caste . . . recruited not by birth but by adoption. Since they could not risk the growth of opposition, and since they silenced criticism, they often made avoidable mistakes; then, because they could not admit that their mistakes were their own, they had to find scapegoats, sometimes on an enormous scale.

In short, throughout his adult life and work, George Orwell remained a fiercely honest man, even with himself. Though he well understood the dangers of socialism, he remained committed to the socialist solution to the political and social problems of the world. He believed that if people understood the dangers, they could avoid them. He knew that socialism meant organization of industry as well as of people, which meant the necessity for further growth of the machine-dependent civilization that he had criticized in *The Road to Wigan Pier* and in *Coming Up for Air*, and that this meant the further destruction of the old country way of life which he loved. He was, however, willing to sacrifice even this if all men could be guaranteed a decent standard of living. He was emphatic that improving man's physical conditions would not solve all man's problems: he believed that the most serious of these problems were not physical but rather spiritual and psychological. But he believed that these more serious problems could not be dealt with until man had conquered his material difficulties — through socialism.

The chief theoretical conflict for Orwell was caused by his awareness of individual human differences, which interfere with the abstract group philosophy of socialism. He was himself a sincere and courageous individualist, and he feared the loss of individual freedom that he knew socialism involved. He was honest enough, despite his awareness, to admit that he saw no answer other than socialism to the world's horrible material problems.

Orwell is often praised for his contribution to making people aware of the dangers of communism. Yet his greatest contribution may turn out to be the lesson he taught about the importance of the individual, so easily threatened by *any* form of dictatorship. This lesson he taught not only by his writings, but by the example of his own person: proud, honest, free and compassionate — no matter what his economic and political beliefs.

Introduction to *1984*

When *1984* was published, a good deal of critical discussion arose over Orwell's purpose in the novel. Some saw it as a prophecy of what was bound to happen to the world; others took it as primarily a comment on contemporary societies; still others looked upon the book as a symptom of the author's sick mind. Judging from his published statements on the matter, Orwell himself seems to have meant the novel to be a criticism of life in the twentieth century as he had experienced it in Burma, Paris and London, Wigan, Barcelona and elsewhere. What has made readers uneasy about it is that Oceania in the year 1984 is but a slight extension of the world as Orwell saw it in 1948.

The book was a success from the time of its first appearance. Millions of copies have been sold around the world, and it has been translated into numerous foreign languages. *1984* is included in courses at both the high-school and university levels.

Many of the terms and concepts created by Orwell for his novel have become part of the vocabulary of the English language — Big Brother, newspeak and doublethink, to name a few. There have been plays, songs and even comic strips which have taken their inspiration from *1984*, and printing after printing of this bleak novel continues to sell out. Few contemporary novels (with the possible exception of Orwell's fable, *Animal Farm*) have succeeded in capturing and holding the imaginations of readers, both young and old. Orwell's final novel, finished soon before his death, remains the crowning achievement of his career.

1984 and Anti-Utopian Fiction

George Orwell's *1984* is, along with Aldous Huxley's *Brave New World*, one of the two great twentieth-century, anti-utopian novels. The tradition of utopian fiction — fiction predicated on the possibility of a perfect existence for man — is very old, as old as the story of the Garden of Eden in Genesis, at least for the Western world. It embodies both nostalgia for a legendary Golden Age and hope for the way man might live in some distant future.

Although The *Republic* of Plato is an older example, the name for this kind of fiction comes from Sir Thomas More's *Utopia*, published in Latin, in 1516. In it, a character discovers a land called Utopia, or Nowhere Land. A popular work, it was translated into English in 1551 and has since served as a model for writers who share More's purpose.The word puns on the Greek *ou topia*, meaning "no place," and *eu topia* or "good place." Utopia has thus come to be the generic name for literature that creates a non-existent ideal government. Plato's *Republic*, Bacon's *The New Atlantis* and Bellamy's *Looking Backward* are utopias.

The nineteenth century was particularly interested in the idea of utopia, both in literature and in actual social experiments. In English literature, there are books such as Samuel Butler's *Erewhon* — "nowhere" spelled backward — (1872) and William Morris' *News from Nowhere* (1891). Tennyson, in "Locksley Hall" (1842), writes of seeing a "Vision of the world" in which man finally learns to live at peace with himself in a "Federation of the world."

In American literature, Edward Bellamy's *Looking Backward* (1888) and Herman Melville's *Typee* (1846) and *Omoo* (1847) are examples of the same impulse to see man in an uncorrupted state. This desire is related to the phenomenon of the frontier in American history. The West allowed the possibility of establishing an ideal society or community free of the historical evils that man had always suffered in Europe. Mark Twain accurately reflects, in *The Adventures of Huckleberry Finn* (1884), the impulse to flee to the frontier and away from civilization. When the peaceful community that Huckleberry Finn and his companion, Jim, establish on the raft is disrupted by the world, Huck eventually decides to "light out for the Territory." This is echoed in our own time in Holden Caulfield's desire to establish a community of the innocent somewhere in the West, in J. D. Salinger's *The Catcher in the Rye*.

Men in the nineteenth century believed in the perfectibility of mankind and in the real possibility of an ultimate utopia, a time when all men would be able to live together in a united world in a state of peace. But, the events of history in the twentieth century have undermined that belief. Both cold and hot wars have followed each other in quick succession. Revolutions and civil wars have clouded the orderly progress of man toward some better future. Totalitarianism has become a fact that can hardly be ignored, from Hitler's Germany to the Russia of Stalin and later Soviet leaders. The doctrine that man can be directed for purposes other than that of developing the best in his nature is, of course, directly opposed to the belief in man's perfectibility. Thus, the modern age has become one in which more anti-utopias are envisioned than ever before.

An anti-utopia is simply the reverse of a conventional utopia. *Gulliver's Travels*, the brilliant eighteenth-century work by Jonathan Swift, is probably the most famous of all anti-utopian novels. The aim of the anti-utopian novel is the same as that of the utopian novel: both have as their objective the improvement of society. The anti-utopian novel, however, instead of presenting an ideal society toward which all men should strive, generally presents a highly defined, completely hideous society. The anti-utopian novel warns that if the tendencies of the real world, exaggerated in the world of fiction, are not corrected before it is too late, the hideous world suggested will become a reality. Orwell's anti-utopia has had a profound influence on our times. Despite the name of the book, *1984* is not a prediction of what the world will be like in 1984; it is, instead, a warning that unless the course in which the world drifts is changed, man will lose his most human attributes. Hence, the choice of its title: 1984 is merely 1948 with two numerals reversed. In a sense, the year 1948 contains the seeds of the anti-utopia of *1984*.

Shortly after writing *Animal Farm*, itself an anti-utopian novel, Orwell published a brief essay on the Russian writer Eugene Zamyatin's *We*, which, although it appeared in 1924, was little known to English-speaking readers. It is said by some critics that there are similarities between *1984* and *We*. Certainly,

11

Orwell was much impressed by the novel, and he read it during the time when he was thinking about his own *1984*. In his essay on *We*, Orwell himself says that it bears some resemblance to Aldous Huxley's *Brave New World* (1932) but, in his opinion, *We* is a better novel.

That three writers in the same time, all interested in the idea of anti-utopia, should produce books with some similarities is hardly a surprise. Of the three, only Orwell's depicts a society whose purpose is solely that of power. For that reason, *1984* has caused more discussion and has made more readers uneasy than either of the other two, although Zamyatin's novel is still not well known to the Western world.

The anti-utopian novel is a specialized branch of fiction. It is true that the author of such a novel is mainly concerned with depicting a certain kind of society. But, since he is writing a novel, by necessity he must use the means available to any novelist: plot, setting, characterization, point of view, structure and the like. To say that he bends these formal aspects to his purpose is only to describe what any good novelist does. The success with which he makes the reader accept the reality he has created is the only meaningful test of his ability as a writer. Orwell, after all, had written several novels before he produced either *Animal Farm* or *1984*. By the time of these later books, he was no longer satisfied with the novel as he had written it and turned to the anti-utopian novel as the most effective means to express his urgent purposes.

Plot Summary

Winston Smith, who works in the Records Department of the Ministry of Truth, revising the past as it appears in newspapers, is dissatisfied living under the inflexible, outwardly paternalistic government of Oceania, epitomized in the ever-present picture of Big Brother. His dissatisfaction is increased by the austerity characteristic of daily life. At first he rebels in small ways. He writes a diary, an act that is viewed with suspicion by the Thought Police, and privately speculates about the political orthodoxy of O'Brien, an important official in the governing Inner Party. He becomes increasingly disturbed by a young woman he finds watching him, and he dreams, over and over, of an idyllic Golden Country, in which sexual expression is as natural as the landscape.

Winston even goes among the proles, the large excluded class, seeking some kind of human contact. The young woman, Julia, initiates a relationship between herself and Winston, and they make love in a scene exactly like that in a dream. He knows that their lovemaking is political in meaning. It is his overt action of rebellion against Oceania, whose policies forbid, or at least control, such activity.

Winston and Julia, their relationship becoming domestic, rent a room to which they can go to be apart from others. Winston and O'Brien meet, the latter taking the initiative, and Winston and Julia together visit O'Brien in his quarters. He leads them to believe he is also in revolt and allows Winston to read an illegal book. Just when Winston is certain that he and Julia will soon be detected — from the beginning he has had little hope they will not be — they are arrested in their rented room. The landlord, an older man, has been a member of the Thought Police all along.

Winston and Julia are imprisoned separately in the Ministry of Love, and Winston is given over to O'Brien for what he learns will be his complete rehabilitation, not immediate execution. By physical and then psychological torture, O'Brien puts Winston through the first two stages of his retraining: learning what is expected of him and, then, understanding it. During the process, Winston comes almost to love O'Brien. Together day after day for nine months, they converse finally as if they were friends.

Preparation for the final stage in Winston's education,

acceptance, comes in the dreaded Room 101, where Winston is made to face what he secretly fears most. Completely subjugated – physically, emotionally, mentally – Winston is then released. Upon the occasion of a threatened attack on Oceania and the defeat of the enemy, Winston feels gratitude and love for Big Brother.

Characters in the Novel

WINSTON SMITH: The male protagonist, 39 years old, thin and blonde, whose personality is destroyed for the major heresy of thoughtcrime after he attempts to challenge the totalitarian system. Employed by the Ministry of Truth, Mini-True, his job is the systematic destruction of past history.

JULIA: The down-to-earth and bold-looking girl of 26. A prominent member of the Junior Anti-Sex League, she runs a novel-writing machine at MiniTrue. After she becomes Winston's mistress, she is brutally punished for this infraction of State-ordained sexual conduct.

O'BRIEN: The Inner Party representative. A large, burly man with a thick neck and a coarse, humorous, brutal face who combines a sophisticated manner with a prizefighter's technique. He acts as the "grand inquisitor" in Winston Smith's destruction.

BIG BROTHER: "Friend of the People." A man of about 45 with a heavy, black mustache and ruggedly handsome features. The Inner Party Leader, he has never been seen in person and quite possibly does not exist except as a fabrication of the Party, his image is constantly projected by all communications media.

EMMANUEL GOLDSTEIN: "Enemy of the People." Once a leading Party figure, almost on level with Big Brother, Goldstein had engaged in counter-revolutionary activities, been condemned to death, mysteriously escaped and disappeared. He is the principal figure in the daily Two Minutes Hate, and he supposedly leads the Brotherhood, a secret organization dedicated to Big Brother's destruction, but which itself is just another fiction manufactured by the Party.

JONES, AARONSON and RUTHERFORD: Three doomed survivors of the original revolutionary leaders, who are tortured and confess to all sorts of imaginary crimes in spectacular public "trials."

THE PARSONS FAMILY: Winston's next-door neighbors at his flat in Victory Mansions. Tom Parsons is Winston's fellow employee at MiniTrue. Reeking from sweat, he is a fat, active man of remarkable stupidity, a completely devoted drudge, the

15

kind of person upon whom Party stability depends. His wife is a woman of about 30, but looks much older. She is terrorized by their children, a son of nine and a daughter of seven, both of whom are members of a youth group, the Spies.

MR. CHARRINGTON: A widower, supposedly 63 years old, and owner of a junky antique shop for 30 years who rents a room to Julia and Winston. Seemingly a link to the almost completely vaporized past, he is actually a Thought Police agent.

KATHARINE: Winston Smith's frigid wife from whom he has been separated 11 years.

SYME: Winston's friend who works in the research department at MiniTrue. A philologist and Newspeak specialist, he is vaporized for ideological inconsistency.

AMPLEFORTH: Another of Winston's working companions at Minitrue. He has a surprising talent for juggling with rhymes and meters. He rewrites garbled versions of past poetry to suit current ideology. He is vaporized for allowing the word "God" to remain at the end of a Kipling poem he is rewriting.

TILLOTSON: A MiniTrue worker in a cubicle on the opposite side of the room from Winston. Tillotson and Winston rewrite the same documents. The Inner Party then chooses the better version.

Chapter by Chapter Summaries and Commentaries

PART I · CHAPTER 1

Summary

Winston Smith, the "hero" of the novel, returns to his seventh-floor flat, from his job at the Ministry of Truth. The Ministry of Truth, or MiniTrue, is one of four government ministries whose towering buildings dominate a war-torn London, the main city of Airstrip One, a province of Oceania. The year is 1984, and the world is divided into three countries permanently at war with each other — Oceania, Eurasia and Eastasia. Oceania is ruled by the Party, whose leader is Big Brother.

Winston is secretly dissatisfied with his life in the decaying city and determines to keep a diary to record his private thoughts and memories. The urge to start a diary, which along with almost everything else is considered a crime in Oceania, had come to Winston during that day's Two Minutes Hate. He had felt his feelings, like everyone else's, being manipulated, during those two minutes, against the Enemy of the Party, Emmanuel Goldstein. Winston had also noticed two people — O'Brien, a Party official, in whose eyes he thought he had seen a sign of common political sympathy, and a young girl whom he instinctively hated due to her embodiment of the traits of athleticism and anti-sex that he disliked in the women of the day.

Winston is aware that it is only a matter of time before his thoughtcrime is detected. A knock at the door brings him out of his reminiscence of recent events. He is afraid, and thinks he has already been discovered.

Commentary

Most of the major ideas, themes and conflicts of *1984* are introduced in this first chapter. Drabness dominates the entire novel. Through the use of euphemism, the Party covers up the drabness with encouraging names. Victory Mansions is a huge tenement of one- and two-room apartments. To conserve electricity for the war effort, power is cut off during the daylight hours. The elevator does not work. There is no running hot water. Yet Winston Smith is a Party member — certainly not one of the Inner Party, but a privileged person nevertheless — and Victory Mansions is rather good housing, especially when contrasted with the buildings in which the non-Party members, the proles, live.

Oceania is one of the three great powers in the world. It consists of the Americas, the British Isles, Australia and a few other territories. The British Isles have been renamed Airstrip One. Winston lives in what remains of London. Old houses, dating back to the nineteenth century, are held up with wooden supports. Windows are patched with cardboard; roofs with corrugated iron. Everywhere there is the rubble of bombed-out buildings. The only modern buildings in the city are the four ministry centers.

The sense of smell is important in establishing the setting. Victory Mansions smells of boiled cabbage and old rag mats, both odors quite unpleasant and both indicative of the squalid conditions in which the members of the Outer Party live. The only way to achieve momentary oblivion is to drink Victory Gin. Everywhere there is the odor of dust and decay.

The figure of Big Brother, spokesman for Party orthodoxy, dominates the psychological setting of *1984*. There is a hint that Big Brother is not even a real person, and the Outer Party members, such as Winston Smith, do not even know where his headquarters are. The indication is that he is merely the symbol of the Party and the State, a figure created to be the subject of the Party members' loyalty and love.

The slogan "Big Brother Is Watching You" is everywhere. There are no laws as such in Oceania, so the citizens always remain fearful that they might do or say, or even think, something harmful to the State and the Party. Not having laws written down serves two purposes for the Party. First, it keeps the citizens fearful and therefore easily controlled. Second, it allows the Party to change policy without having to admit that it has changed.

The concept of doublethink is important in the psychological makeup of the characters in *1984*. In its simplest application, doublethink makes it possible to refer to a miserable tenement building as "Victory" Mansions and a cheap bitter synthetic as "Victory" Coffee. In its more sophisticated application, doublethink makes possible the three major slogans of Oceania. The only way that Oceania can exist as a state is for it to wage a constant war — the whole structure of society and state is geared to wartime economy and austerity. If there should be peace, the citizens of Oceania might reasonably expect better living conditions, better food and less control by the government. To convince everyone in Oceania that war is the best state possible for them, the state has developed the slogan WAR IS PEACE. And the minds of the Party members have been so conditioned that, with an occasional rare exception, everyone sees the slogan as perfectly logical.

Freedom of thought and expression is dangerous to a totalitarian state. It is necessary, therefore, that the citizens of the state be made to think that deviation from orthodox thought and expression enslaves the man who allows it: FREEDOM IS SLAVERY.

The right to question and to learn is also dangerous to the state. Party members, except those at the very highest levels, must remain as ignorant as little children so that they may be easily led in the way in which they should go: IGNORANCE IS STRENGTH.

Citizens of Oceania are not allowed to respond intellectually to their government. Their only response must be emotional. They must love Big Brother, with all the trust that love implies, and they must hate the enemy, whether it be the traitor and potential saboteur, Emmanuel Goldstein, or one of the two other superstates, Eurasia or Eastasia. To bind the Party members closely to the State, there is the frequent Two Minutes Hate period. Winston Smith has intellectual doubts about this period. However, the way that the propaganda is handled is so effective that, despite his doubts, Winston frequently feels the emotions that he is supposed to feel. His response puzzles him, and this puzzlement is one of the reasons for his intellectual and emotional uneasiness.

The person of Emmanuel Goldstein is another important psychological factor in *1984*. He questioned whether constant war was beneficial or indeed necessary, as the Party taught. His book struck at the foundations of Party philosophy. It was unique in that it alone, unlike all the written material available to Party members and proles, was written with historical perspective.

It is historically significant that Orwell should have chosen a Jewish name for the person of the defector. Less than a decade before the 1949 publication of *1984*, half of Europe had been engaged in an attempt to exterminate all the Jews on the sub-continent. These unfortunate people had been accused of all kinds of political — as well as economic and social — unortho-doxy. The Brotherhood, as the organization which Goldstein was supposed to have headed was called, remained underground and waited its chance to overthrow the Party. It is interesting to note that one of the Hebrew words used as a name for the Messiah — the great political and religious leader who was to rise up among them to lead them to freedom — is Emmanuel. The surname "Goldstein" is a possible reference to the money-grubbing character which all Jews were supposed to have.

Outwardly, Winston Smith is an efficient and orthodox member of the Outer Party. Inwardly, Winston is troubled. He vaguely remembers how things were before the Party took con-trol — nothing concrete at this point, only vague flashes of scenes. More seriously, he has begun to doubt the collective wisdom of the Party.

Winston has begun to wonder about the nature of history and of truth. To the orthodox Party member, such questions and speculations would never arise. What the Party states as truth now has always been true and will be true forever. What it states as truth tomorrow has, likewise, always been true and will always be true. Winston knows differently, however.

Winston becomes obsessed with a desire to pin down truth, to fix it in some way that cannot be changed later by the Ministry of Truth. It is for this reason — which he only vaguely under-stands himself — that he begins to write.

Winston's reaction to the Hate period is interesting, and it shows the essential double nature of his position. Realizing in-tellectually that he is being manipulated by the propaganda, he is nevertheless caught up in the emotional experience of hate. He is fascinated by Goldstein, however, and turns his hate toward the young woman and toward Big Brother. He hates as he is supposed to hate, but he hates the wrong people.

Orwell possibly intended Winston Smith's name to have significance. The most vital and influential man in England in the mid-twentieth century was, of course, Winston Churchill. It seems certain that Orwell intended an ironic contrast in giving an ineffectual member of the Outer Party this first name. This irony is further enforced by the addition of the surname, Smith, the most common family name in the English-speaking world. In a sense, Winston Smith represents Everyman. However, he deviates from the common man's ordinary tendency to accept things as he is told to accept them. In this deviation, he rises above the ordinary, unthinking members of the Party around him.

Although Winston does not know her name, he is both fascinated and repelled by the young woman, Julia. Winston hates her type, the sexually attractive young women who are usually the most faithful followers of the Party line and who sometimes act as spies for the Thought Police. He realizes the danger of betraying any interest in her whatsoever.

During the Hate period, Winston's hatred turns from the enemies of the State to Julia, whom he considers his personal enemy. Yet, at the same time, the reader is aware that Winston loves Julia, that his fantasy is the result of frustration, not of real hate.

Since Winston has begun to have his doubts about the Party, he has sought a person with whom to share them. He thinks he has found one in O'Brien. However, it is extremely dangerous for Winston to approach a fellow human being. If he is wrong about O'Brien's attitude toward the Party, he might have to answer to the Thought Police.

The most obvious theme of *1984* is, of course, political. Orwell is implicitly criticizing the kind of government that attempts to control the intellect and emotions of its citizens. Although he has not fully described the government of Oceania in this first chapter, he has given sufficient clues to indicate the most serious shortcomings of a totalitarian state: the all-pervasive character of government and the lack of freedom of dissent. Not only is there no freedom of speech, there is no freedom of thought. The furtiveness with which Winston Smith records his as yet unformed thoughts pointedly shows this lack of freedom. What the reader learns of the workings of the Ministry of Truth and the Ministry of Love — with its Thought Police enforcement — is terrifying. The reader — himself in search of truth — is drawn immediately to identify with Winston Smith in the latter's search. Immediately, the reader sees Winston committing a treasonable act: thinking unorthodoxly and even daring to write down his thoughts. Thus, suspense is introduced. The reader realizes — if only vaguely — what will happen to Winston when he is found out, as he certainly must be found out.

There are also two other important and interrelated themes established in this first chapter. The first of these is the inability of a man to communicate his thoughts fully to another human being. Winston's most pressing psychological problem is not his doubting the infallibility of the State, but the fact that there is no one with whom he can communicate this doubt and discuss it. He wishes desperately to see a kindred spirit in the person of O'Brien, an intelligent member of the Inner Party. Winston is not able to decide whether O'Brien is showing real signs of unorthodoxy, or whether Winston himself is only seeing what he wants to see.

There is also the lack of intellectual and emotional communication expressed in Winston's attitude toward Julia. He lusts after her, both physically and emotionally, but she is a member of a girls' political organization devoted to purity to the point of frigidity. We learn later that Winston has been married in the past. Even in that unsatisfactory marriage, he has learned something of the companionship that can be present in marriage. His hatred for Julia is the necessary reversal of what he actually feels toward her. Since he feels that he cannot have her, it is necessary for him to hate her.

Inability to communicate inevitably results in frustration, and this frustration is another important theme in the novel. It is frustration as much as anything else that motivates Winston Smith. He cannot understand and he cannot ask anyone to help him understand. So, he must take out his frustration in writing and in the fantasies of the Two Minutes Hate. Orwell also mirrors Winston Smith's emotional discomfort in the physical discomfort of the itching varicose ulcer. All aspects of his life torment him.

Notes

varicose ulcer: Obviously, Winston is in poor physical shape. This is an ulcer caused by deterioration of the veins, usually on the legs or feet.

the Party: Since Oceania is ruled by a single party that allows no opposition, there is no need to specify *which* party.

Ingsoc: The Newspeak term for "English Socialism." The name is typical of Newspeak, in that by reduction, the word carries very little meaning.

Newspeak: The official language of Oceania. See Appendix to *1984*.

nothing was illegal: Because there are no specific laws, the Party is able to rule absolutely, with no appeal to a body of law open to interpretation by its victims.

prole: short for "proletarian." Proles make up 85% of Oceania's population, but are considered by the Party as little more than beasts. They are the working class.

Goldstein: possibly modelled after Leon Trotsky, who had been exiled and then murdered as a result of political disagreement with Stalin, the Russian leader.

It was always at night: Winston knows what his eventual fate will be. The practice of secret, nighttime arrests is typical of secret police in a totalitarian state, and is meant to create terror, not only in the person arrested, but also in those around him.

CHAPTER 2

Summary

Mrs. Parsons, a neighbor, is there when Winston opens the door, and she asks him to unblock her sink. He does so, but is repelled by the smell of sweat that is everywhere in the Parsons' apartment. Mr. Parsons is a mindless follower of Party doctrine and a fellow employee at MiniTrue. The two Parsons children are members of the Spies, a Party youth organization which encourages spying on and denunciation of "traitors," including their own parents. Winston is revolted by this also.

He returns to his apartment and writes for a few more minutes before realizing it is time to return to work. He had been remembering a dream he had had in which O'Brien told him he would meet him "in the place where there is no darkness." He carefully washes his hands of ink and hides the diary in such a way that he will know if it has been disturbed during his absence. He is aware that the Thought Police will be the only other readers of it.

Commentary

Although he does not actually come into the narrative until later, Tom Parsons is discussed in this chapter. He is intended to be something of a foil character to Winston, that is, a character to which Winston is consciously or unconsciously contrasted. Tom Parsons is a stupid, family man, who swallows whole everything that the party feeds him.

Tom Parsons would never think of questioning the Party in its collective wisdom. He does not work for the Party out of fear or even out of a sense of duty; he works for the Party because he enjoys it. This unthinking, animalistic enthusiast, Orwell seems to be saying, is the only kind of man for whom the kind of government that exists in Oceania is suited.

The dream is important to the full revelation of Winston Smith's character. The dream can operate on two levels, emotional and intellectual. On the emotional level, Winston is looking for a guide, something of a father figure, to lead him to security. The voice in the dream is the kind and helpful voice of such a fatherly guide. On the intellectual level, the darkness of the room may represent the ignorance that Winston feels himself lost in, since black is frequently associated with not knowing.

The knowledge that he does not conform is uppermost in Winston's mind in this chapter. The Parsons are a family of conformists, and Winston is shown to be acutely aware that he is different from them. He is not happy, he is not even mildly satisfied, in conformity. It is evident from a remark entered in his diary that he hopes for a time when men are different, but 1984 is a time of conformity, when nothing is private but the individual human brain. And even that, it is vaguely hinted, is not safe.

Notes

discountenanced: out of sorts, disturbed, upset.

invertebrate: spineless, undecided.

salt mines: During the purges in Russia, thousands of dissidents were sent to Siberia to labor in the mines. Many died there due to hard labor and poor working conditions.

the place where there is no darkness: This foreshadows the meeting in Part III, Chapter 1, in which Winston and O'Brien do meet, in the well-lit torture room of the Ministry of Love.

mutability: changeability.

CHAPTER 3

Summary

Waking from disturbing dreams of his mother and sister, Winston vaguely remembers their disappearance and feels, equally vaguely, that he was somehow responsible for their deaths. His second dream had been of an idyllic countryside, and a girl resembling the one he had noticed at the Two Minutes Hate. In the dream, she had stripped off her clothes for him in a very sensual and yet natural way.

It is the two-way telescreen that had caused Winston to wake up, as usual, in order for him to take part in compulsory strenuous exercises. While undergoing these painful exertions, he thinks about the absolute control that the Party holds over all information. His thoughts are interrupted by the comment of the instructress on the telescreen, who praises his next attempts to exercise.

Commentary

The Golden Country of Winston's dream obviously represents freedom from the drabness of London, and even more importantly, freedom from the always present Party, the Thought Police and Big Brother. This time, however, the dream takes a slightly different turn.

Winston's memory of his parents and his little sister is colored by guilt and regret. He knows now how selfish he was as a child and is sorry that he passed up his chance to let his parents, especially his mother, know that he loved them, at a time when the word "love" still meant something.

The question of history is intimately tied up with Winston's search for truth. The fact that Winston remembers a different alliance of the three countries bothers him, but he is still thinking in terms of the Party line somewhat when he dismisses it. Yet, the power of the Party over history is frightening to Winston.

As Winston sees further evidence of the power of the State and the inconsequential nature of the individual in such a State, he becomes more and more disturbed. The personal values of love, honor and family loyalty have been utterly rooted out and destroyed by the Party. All rational codes of behavior have been replaced by blind, emotional loyalty to Big Brother, who alone has the power to create and to destroy. Winston realizes the treason of even questioning these things in his mind, but he cannot control his waking thoughts and especially the thoughts of his sleep, his dreams.

As yet, he has been unable to formulate the problem fully and is certainly in no position to begin thinking along lines that might lead to a solution. There is the feeling that *something* must happen, that he cannot go on as he has the last few days.

Notes

purge: A "purge" is an elimination of people considered undesirable by the ruling party.

the Golden Country: The dream stands in stark contrast to the decaying urban landscape that constitutes the bleak reality of Winston's world.

gyrating: turning back and forth.

capitalists: those who have accumulated "capital" or wealth derived from the work of others. This is then used to produce more "capital." A term of Marxist analysis.

CHAPTER 4

Summary

Winston begins the day's work at the Ministry of Truth. His job is to correct printed articles in line with the Party's orders. The Ministry and, in particular, its Records Department, are described in great detail. Basically, their task is to rewrite history in order to make the Party look infallible. The Two Minutes Hate provides a break, after which Winston replaces a speech by Big Brother with an invented history of a fictional Comrade Ogilvy. This is done because the speech in the newspaper files has become contrary to present Party policy. It is replaced as if it had never existed.

Commentary

Two items are important in this chapter: the nature of Winston Smith's work in the Records Department of the Ministry of Truth and Winston's attitude toward his job.

Although Winston knows that the Records Department of the Ministry of Truth is engaged in altering historical accounts, he frequently enjoys his work. Intellectually, he realizes that the record of past history should be the same from day to day. Nevertheless, he feels that the lies which he writes in his work are not important lies. Actually, the greatest pleasure in his life is the work that he does at the Records Department. It is often a challenge. Winston, because he likes his work and because he has a certain flair for it, is good, and, on occasion, his superiors allow him to rewrite even the lead stories in the *Times*, which have to be worded entirely in Newspeak.

Notes

orifices: openings of the body, such as the mouth or ears.

ideological: having to do with ideas of a particular political or economic theory.

palimpsest: an erased manuscript, used a second time for a different text.

repositories: places of safekeeping.

abstainer: a non-drinker.

CHAPTER 5

Summary

Winston meets Syme, a philologist, for lunch. Syme explains certain facets of Newspeak, before they are joined by Parsons. Winston, thinking of the fate awaiting each of these co-workers, concludes that Syme is too intelligent and will be vaporized, and that Parsons is dull enough to escape vaporization. Winston also concludes that everyone but he has been taken in by the propaganda constantly being broadcast. He notices that the same girl from the previous day's Two Minutes Hate is at another table and is staring at him. Uncomfortable, he is afraid she is a member of the dreaded Thought Police.

Commentary

The basic principle of Newspeak is the destruction of words, the stripping of language to the barest elements. All shadings in the meanings of words are also destroyed. Thus, theoretically, a word will mean exactly the same thing to all the people using it. In addition, all concepts not in line with Party philosophy are utterly destroyed, so that in a generation's time, when all people use nothing but Newspeak, it will be impossible to have a thoughtcrime. One will not be able to form an idea against the Party, since no words will exist for unorthodox ideas. The eventual aim of Newspeak is to narrow the range of thought until eventually there will *be* no thought.

Keeping his opinion hidden from everyone around him, Winston reflects bitterly that the physical things of life in Oceania are not what they should be. The food, drink and tobacco are unappealing. Living conditions are primitive and unwholesome. All elements of life are coarse. And yet, Winston cannot himself remember things ever having been any better. He wonders why he has the idea that they could be.

The point of Winston's wondering about the effectiveness of the Party's propaganda involves "the mutability of the past." This whole question forms one of the bases of the entire plot. The Party is in the act of abolishing the past: it carefully alters facts to

27

suit its current situation. That is Winston's task at the Ministry of Truth: to alter the past to suit the present. Winston's memory retains facts and fragments of facts which do not agree with the present facts of the Party. For example, he remembers that in the past the enemy has changed a number of times, but the Party at the moment claims that Eurasia has always been the enemy. He is also, in the course of his work, required to revise a promise about the chocolate ration. Winston is disturbed by the fact that the Party can literally decide that an event has not occurred and that the very act of saying it removes the event from history.

The same is true of individuals. Persons who have been purged by the Party, if they are referred to at all, are known as "unpersons," because they do not exist and never have. All reference to them is purged along with them. Winston's diary will not survive him, and he will cease to exist, like any other unperson. To Winston, this is far worse than torture and death.

Notes
philologist: an expert in linguistics, the science of words.
synonyms: words with equivalent meanings.
antonyms: words of opposite meanings.
there is a war on: justification for continuous shortages of all
    kinds.
B.B.: Big Brother.

CHAPTER 6

Summary
Winston records in his diary an encounter several years before with a prostitute made up to look young, but who was in reality a withered hag. His memory of the encounter causes him to think of the policy regarding sex and marriage fostered by the Party. This, in turn, causes him to think of his unsatisfactory life with Katharine, the wife he has not seen in eleven years. Winston resents the intrusion of the Party into the sex lives of its members and realizes that the Party's discouragement of sexual enjoyment makes any love affair with a Party member impossible for him. Unfortunately, writing down the incident with the prostitute does not relieve him of its horror.

Commentary
Because the sexual act often leads to an emotional bond between people, a loyalty which the Party cannot control, the

Party discourages sexual relationships among its members. Party members are allowed to marry only if they show no physical attraction to each other. Intercourse between married people is looked upon as an unpleasant necessity which must be performed occasionally in order to have children. Many zealous Party members, especially those belonging to the Junior Anti-Sex League, vow celibacy, wanting nothing to do with anything that might take their thoughts and energies away from their Party duties. Only the proles are left free to live together and enjoy sex for its own sake.

In this chapter, there is an interesting example of the acuteness of Winston's sensibilities. The only memory connected with the prostitute that he still finds exciting is the scent of a cheap perfume that she wore. Of course, only prole women are allowed to wear scent, and only they were allowed to enjoy the sex act. Winston then associates the cheap perfume with freedom. The therapy of confessing in his diary his last sexual experience does not work for Winston. He still longs for the kind of sexual experience which is no longer possible in the society in which he lives.

CHAPTER 7

Summary

Winston makes another entry in his diary, this one concerning the proles. He feels that only they have any power that might overthrow the Party, but that they are unaware of it. There is no possibility of recovering the truth of the past, as a result of all records being controlled by the Party, but Winston instinctively feels that life in the present is worse than before. He remembers a photograph that happened to come into his possession. It proved that the Party was intent on falsifying the past, but he destroyed it.

Looking to the future, Winston fears a time when the Party will declare that two plus two equals five. He plans to hold stubbornly to self-evident truths, in order to keep some form of freedom.

Commentary

Winston has faith in the proles, and in their ability to revolt. However, there is no indication that the masses ever revolt by themselves. Leadership is usually required. In Oceania, in which any potential leadership is immediately rooted out by the Thought Police and any divergence from orthodox behavior is not tolerated, that leadership is not likely to develop. O'Brien will have a number of interesting things to say about this possibility when he instructs Winston in Party doctrine.

Orwell is presenting in a fictional form the disillusionment with Soviet Communism that came with Stalin's great purge of the 1930s. Winston remarks that of the original Party leaders of the Revolution, only Big Brother remains. After the purging of the Soviet Communist Party, only Stalin, of all the original revolutionaries, remained in a position of power in Russia. His potential opposition had been swept away. Some Western liberals had admired what they mistakenly believed Soviet Communism to be. They were horrified, however, at the injustice of the Party trials in the 1930s and most of them lost faith in the Russian system as a result.

If truth lies in the mind of the individual, and if the Party can control the mind of the individual, how can there be any truth outside the official Party version of things? This question bothers Winston. He, as an individual, knows at least one lie that the Party has passed off as truth, yet he is helpless to prove that lie except in his own mind. Since everyone but he seems to accept the lie, is he alone insane? After reflection on the subject, he comes to the conclusion that he is indeed sane, and that there are certain unchangeable truths outside the jurisdiction of the Party and that he must hold on to these truths.

Notes

indoctrinate: to instruct, to force someone to learn.

sinecures: jobs that involve no work, yet for which someone is paid. Usually given as a reward for loyalty of one kind or another.

stratum: a layer of material among many such layers.

arrayed: laid out, arranged.

axiom: an assumption taken as self-evident. Upon an axiom, further premises are built.

CHAPTER 8

Summary

After work one evening, Winston wanders into a prole section of London, unintentionally ending up near the shop in which he had bought his diary. He follows an old man into a prole pub, with a vague desire to ask him what things had been like before the Revolution. The old man is incoherent. Winston leaves the prole pub and wanders. He ends up outside the antique shop again and goes in to buy a glass paperweight. The owner, Mr. Charrington, shows him a room upstairs filled with old furniture and, for a moment, Winston daydreams of renting it. On leaving the shop, he notices the dark-haired girl watching him. When he gets home, he is certain she belongs to the Thought Police and that his arrest is imminent. He thinks, despairingly, that there is no escape from the life imposed by the Party.

Commentary

In this chapter, a crisis is reached. Winston makes a physical, as contrasted to an intellectual, break with orthodoxy. He disregards the danger of detection by the Thought Police.

"Ownlife" is a Newspeak word meaning individualism and eccentricity. Since it means deviation, however slight, from the accepted social form, it is dangerous to the State. Winston is in danger of being noticed as an eccentric and brought to the attention of the Thought Police.

The "oranges and lemons" rhyme, introduced in this chapter, gains significance as the book progresses. It is a child's game, played in the same way as "London Bridge Is Falling Down."

Winston's recurring dream, in which the voice of O'Brien promises that they shall meet, is connected symbolically to this children's rhyme. O'Brien seems to say that he is bringing a candle to light Winston to bed (that is, security), when in reality he turns out to be a torturer.

Notes

anodyne: a drug to kill pain temporarily.

His voice was soft: This is an indication that Mr. Charrington is not a prole. Winston does not follow this line of reasoning, but dismisses it.

lassitude: fatigue.

knell: the sounding of a bell. Often used to suggest the coming of death or disaster.

PART II · CHAPTER 1

Summary

At work, Winston encounters the dark-haired girl again, this time in a hallway. She falls and, while he is lifting her, he is surprised to find that she has slipped him a piece of paper. On reading it, back at his desk, he is amazed at her message, which states simply: "I love you."

Eager to arrange a meeting with her, Winston has to wait several days until they eat together in the cafeteria. A meeting in crowded Victory Square is finally arranged. That evening in the Square, the girl instructs Winston how and where to meet her the next Sunday afternoon.

Commentary

Winston's readiness to enter into a relationship, to accept Julia's advances at face value rather than to question them as a possible trap, indicates that he is ready for thought crime. His dissatisfaction with life and his sexual frustration make him ripe for the occasion.

In terms of the inevitable conclusion of events, this section may be considered the beginning of the end. By allowing himself to be drawn into the adventure, Winston is condemning himself. Although at the close of Part I he is ready for thoughtcrime, he might still have drawn back. When he accepts the girl's advances, he is completely doomed. At the moment when he reads the note, it becomes important for him to remain alive, not to take unnecessary risks. But at the same instant, the risk no longer matters. This is another instance of Winston's duality of mind. This state of mind will characterize him throughout the entire second part. To put it another way, Winston has learned to hope, but he has learned to hope at the very moment when he has placed himself in a hopeless situation. It is important to notice that the girl herself is only a means by which Winston is trying to change his situation.

The most significant elements of Julia's personality, revealed in this chapter, are her vitality and her natural aggressiveness. It is she who makes the overture to Winston, and it is she who plans their future meetings. Although it is Winston who takes the lead in their flight from intellectual orthodoxy, it is Julia who leads in their flight from physical repression.

Orwell may have intended some significance in choosing the name Julia for her heroine. The name seems to suggest Juliet, one of the famous heroines in the literature of romance. Juliet defied authority to be with her lover, as does Julia to be with hers. Other than this one similarity, all comparison is ironic, as the meaningfulness of the world in *Romeo and Juliet* is very different from the meaninglessness of Winston's world in *1984*.

Notes

mated: a chess term, meaning a final defeat.
fluted: ridged, like a seashell.
scrimmage: used here to indicate a confused scramble.

CHAPTER 2

Summary

At the designated meeting place, in the countryside outside London, Winston finally learns the girl's name. Julia explains that she considers herself thoroughly corrupt, and that she has had sex with many Outer Party members, while keeping up a front of Anti-Sex League activity.

Walking, Winston comes upon a scene which exactly matches the idyllic Golden Country of his dreams. Winston and Julia return to the clearing, Julia removes her clothes just like the girl in his dream, and they make love.

Winston is consoled by the existence of such indiscriminate sexual desire, because he sees it as a possible undermining force which could destroy the complete control which the Party exercises over people's lives.

Commentary

Instead of being disappointed that Julia is not a virgin, Winston is happy to find that she has had previous affairs. He sees the only hope for man in the corruption of the Party from within, since the proles can never overthrow the Party from without. His opinion about their ability to revolt has changed from Part I, Chapter 7. Ironically, Winston has turned corruption into something desirable. Julia's sexual freedom is corruption as far as the Party is concerned, but it is desirable as far as human relationships are important. The corruption of the Party's dehumanizing code is the only salvation of the human being.

The irony of the lovemaking Winston and Julia give themselves to is important. At this point, so close to the event, Winston is not aware of the irony. He will realize it much later. But, the reader should recognize its significance. The irony stems from Winston's need to live and his involvement in life occurring exactly at the moment when his time is short because of the very nature of the rebellious act itself. The paradox of life and death, of seeing and not seeing, of madness and sanity is thematically important to the book.

Everything before the idyllic scene in the woods leads up to it, and everything that follows stems from it. In short, this may be considered one of the climaxes of the book. The main climax, however, comes at the end of Part II, and there is a third in the last part. If the movement of the book is conceived of as a series of three overlapping curves, this scene marks the peak of the first curve. These three curves may also be said to represent the three major themes of the book. The first of these themes is physical (erotic) love. The second theme is physical pain rather than love, and the last is psychological destruction or change.

Notes

ring-doves: a variety of bird. This entire chapter is filled with references to nature.

etiolated: unhealthily pale due to lack of sun.

obeisance: a bow or other form of respectful greeting.

CHAPTER 3

Summary

Following their first secret meeting, Winston and Julia are able to meet again occasionally. Julia takes charge and arranges the meetings. They next make love in a deserted church. The number of obligatory "voluntary" activities connected with their work prevents them from meeting during the month of May, but they see each other after that whenever they can.

In their discussions during these meetings, it becomes clear that Julia does not share Winston's views on rebellion against the Party. She advises outward obedience and compliance with the Party's doctrine, and breaking the rules, in secret, whenever possible. Unlike Winston, she does not feel a sense of doom due to her private disobedience. They discuss previous relationships which they have had. Julia explains her interpretation of the Party's denial of sex. Deprivation of sex leads to an inner hysteria, and this reaction can then be channelled by the Party into the hysteria of the Two Minutes Hate and blind love of Big Brother. It is another method of mind control.

Commentary

It has been about two months since Winston and Julia first met. In less than a year, Winston's whole history will be over. Both of them, while conscious that they are bringing the end nearer, are unaware of what, exactly, the future holds. They expect to be arrested, to be tortured, to be killed. They do not expect the full horror of what will happen. They are, for the moment, living in a false paradise.

On the one hand, Julia is completely adapted to escape detection in the complex society in which she lives but, on the other, she is almost an earth goddess committed to the animal-physical joy of living. It is an irony that such a woman should be the immediate cause of death and destruction. She demonstrates to Winston with the warmth of her own body her unthinking conviction that they are far from dead. She has hope. And she tries to teach Winston to hope or at least to believe in some kind of possible future.

But, Julia lives from day to day, from sexual encounter to sexual encounter. She is not concerned with the kinds of ideas that trouble Winston. She is concerned with the immediate causes of living, not with the abstract causes of dying. Her view of the world, of course, is just as unrealistic and just as dualistic as Winston's, but from quite a different starting point.

Notes

it was inconceivable: At this point, Winston has not seriously considered renting the room Mr. Charrington had showed him.

loosestrife: a plant common along roads and ditches.

We are the dead: Variations on this expression occur several more times in the novel. It is extremely effective in conveying a tone of bleakness and fatalism.

CHAPTER 4

Summary

Winston eventually does rent the room above Mr. Charrington's antique shop, though he is aware of the foolishness of what he and Julia are doing. The room is full of antique furniture, and Julia arrives bringing contraband real coffee and real sugar, and also old-fashioned makeup. She examines the glass paperweight and other decorations in the room and chases away a rat that has entered through a hole in the woodwork. Winston admits that rats terrify him more than anything else. As Julia tries to remember an old nursery rhyme, Winston meditates on the paperweight and imagines that he, Julia and the room itself are enclosed within it.

Commentary

Winston, under the influence of Julia, is slowly drifting toward a more physical orientation. Having lived in celibacy for nearly a dozen years and having had virtually no sex life during his marriage, he is emotionally immature. His immaturity displays itself in this situation. Winston is a case of arrested development. Now that he has been freed to develop, his view of the world will become more unrealistic. Already, he is extending, in his imagination, the possible length of his relationship with Julia. In actuality, of course, they have very little time.

Several symbols of importance appear in this section. The most striking, immediately, is the glass paperweight. For Winston, it becomes a miniature world in which he can see himself and Julia safe from change and from life under Big Brother. The print of St. Clement's and the nursery rhyme about London churches remind him of the past, which is important both to him and to the Party, but in different ways. Winston's fear of rats, mentioned here so unobtrusively, seems unimportant at the moment. In fact, the meaning of all these symbols will change greatly in later incidents.

Notes

the glass paperweight in the half-darkness: Here, the paperweight comes to represent the relationship between Winston and Julia. Hidden in the darkness, it gleams.

fender: a baffle placed in front of a heat source to deflect sparks and to diffuse the heat.

wainscotting: the baseboard along the foot of the wall.

countersign: password.

CHAPTER 5

Summary

The many preparations for the upcoming Hate Week keep Winston, Julia and the others very busy. Winston discovers that Syme has disappeared and that all records of his very existence have been altered. Meanwhile, the dull Parsons is extremely busy and happy in Hate Week preparations. Winston's premonition about the fate of the two men has been correct.

Due to the increased workload, Julia and Winston meet infrequently, but as often as they can, at the room above the antique shop. Mr. Charrington shows Winston items from the past and they discuss nursery rhymes and other forbidden things.

Winston and Julia discuss the hopelessness of their private rebellion. They both realize it cannot go on forever. Winston is disappointed to find that Julia does not reject much of the Party's propaganda. He accuses her, in a friendly way, of being a rebel only from the waist down. She surprises him, though, with her theory that the bombs that fall on London are not launched by the enemy, but from within Oceania by the Party, as another way of manipulating the people into a mood of war.

Commentary

This chapter is important for its continuation of the differentiation of the characters of Winston and Julia. It is important to note that Orwell seems to be implying that the totalitarian state satisfies neither the intellectual nor the physically oriented pleasure-seeker.

Julia's understanding of the ways in which Party ideas work is much keener than Winston's, although she accepts unthinkingly much of its mythology. She believes that the Party invented airplanes and that Oceania has always been at war with Eurasia. The whole business of abstract truth does not concern her. Winston tells her about the incident when he held the scrap of evidence in his hand, but Julia does not understand the episode. In short, Winston and Julia fall into a pattern of cliché-ridden domesticity: the husband makes all the important decisions about national policy, religious doctrine, space exploration and the like, while the wife makes all the trivial decisions about where the next vacation will be spent, how the family money will be used and so on. Julia is practical while Winston is something of an idealist and a dreamer.

Orwell's intention is obvious. He wants these two rebels to appear to be very ordinary people. And they are. They are essentially middle-class people with ordinary middle-class desires and needs. They do not really wish to change the world in any radical way. They just want to be left alone to live out their own lives peacefully and quietly. One of the horrors of Oceania is that fulfilment of their wish is quite out of the question.

Notes

Syme: Winston had predicted his disappearance in Part I, Chapter 5.

effigies: models made, which carry the image of real people.

febrile: shaky and fevered.

pinchbeck: a type of metal that looks like gold.

CHAPTER 6

Summary

One day at work, O'Brien strikes up a conversation with Winston. They chat, and O'Brien gives Winston his address and asks him to drop by so that O'Brien can lend him an advance copy of the Newspeak dictionary. Winston interprets this friendly gesture of O'Brien's as proof that he is being invited to join in a conspiracy against the Party. Winston looks forward to this, although he foresees that it will undoubtedly end in his torture and death, at the hands of the Party.

Commentary

Winston defines his rebellion in three steps, taken at long intervals over a period of years: first, an unorthodox thought; second, an unorthodox word, the diary; and third, an unorthodox act, his relationship with Julia and the upcoming visit with O'Brien. He accepts the fourth step, his arrest and torture in the Ministry of Love, as inevitable; but he is too excited by O'Brien's attentions toward him to worry much about the eventual outcome.

At this point in the novel, Winston, and the reader, see O'Brien as a kind and pleasant man. Unlike other members of the Inner Party, he is not condescending in his remarks to Winston, even as he praises him for his work.

CHAPTER 7

Summary

Winston dreams of his mother again. This time, he remembers the hunger and stressful conditions that were in existence prior to her disappearance. He is overwhelmed with guilt due to his memories of having always demanded extra amounts of the rationed food, and his having stolen his sister's chocolate. When he returned from eating it in hiding, his mother and sister had disappeared.

Winston tries to tell Julia about his dream, but she is too sleepy to really listen. They later discuss the future and the form their punishment will take, and Winston concludes that though the Party tries to destroy all feeling between human beings, it cannot change what is inside of him. He is glad that it cannot change how he feels about Julia, as that would be the ultimate betrayal.

Commentary

In remembering the events of his childhood, Winston realizes exactly why his mother had been such an admirable person. She was not unusual or even intelligent but had nobility and purity, because the standards she obeyed were private ones. She had been allowed to have feelings and to follow them, a thing impossible to a Party member in 1984.

Winston's belief that no matter what happens to him he can resist in his inner self is perhaps the greatest irony in the book, since the last third of the novel is a detailed treatise on exactly how the Party does get inside an individual, just exactly how his betrayal of himself can be effected, and just exactly how he is able not only to rationalize the fact that he has given himself away, but come to love the person who has caused him to betray himself.

In this section, Winston resolves his guilt feelings about his youth and about his relationship with his mother. But more important, he raises the question of resisting the Party by keeping his innermost self untouched. This belief creates a tension that makes it easy to anticipate the sort of punishment he will face for unorthodox behavior.

CHAPTER 8

Summary

Winston takes Julia with him on his promised visit to O'Brien's apartment. His conviction that O'Brien is also a rebel wavers when they find him hard at work, but O'Brien turns off his telescreen and explains, over a toast to Goldstein, what is required of those that join the secret rebel Brotherhood. Winston and Julia both accept all of the terms of membership except for the requirement that they never see each other again.

O'Brien promises Winston that he will be given a copy of Emmanuel Goldstein's book, secretly, sometime in the near future.

Commentary

Winston sees O'Brien as a strong, unexcitable man. He is efficient, and he appears to be dedicated wholeheartedly to the Brotherhood. Physically, he is massive and ugly, but his physical characteristics suit well his overall appearance of strength and determination.

In a highly ironic exchange, O'Brien outlines the methods of the Brotherhood: murder, slaughter, sabotage, forgery, blackmail, the corruption of children, the spreading of narcotics and venereal diseases, suicide. All are intended to corrupt the Party, a goal which Winston has discussed at length in Chapter 2 of Part II. Also, it is easy to see that these methods are much the same as those used by the Party to keep its members and the proles under control. Winston is exchanging one horror for another; but he sees at the end of the second horror, after generations of struggle, the eventual overthrow of the Party and the triumph of the individual. He has agreed with the dangerous view that the ends justify the means.

As Winston leaves, O'Brien begins to speak of meeting him again, and Winston volunteers the phrase from his dream. O'Brien, obviously not surprised, agrees. Since O'Brien should have had no way of knowing the phrase from Winston's dream, the reader is put on guard by his response. In a short time, the "place where there is no darkness" will take on quite a different meaning from the one that Winston intends.

Notes

persiflage: idle conversation in an ironic tone.

demur: disagreement.

We are the dead: Note the recurrence of this phrase, as well as the image from Winston's dream — the place where there is no darkness. The presence of both here indicates the dramatic importance of this meeting.

equivocal: ambiguous.

CHAPTER 9

Summary

After an exhausting week, in which millions of documents have had to be altered to prove the Party's decision that Eastasia, and not Eurasia, was the enemy they had been fighting all along, Winston rushes to the rented room with the copy of Goldstein's book. He reads it eagerly and afterward lies back to enjoy the relaxation of the moment. Julia falls asleep when he tries to read her sections of it.

Commentary

In various isolated statements throughout the novel, Orwell gives something of the psychology of Hate Week. To drain the energies of the Party members and the proles alike, energies that might be turned toward individual discontent with living conditions, in general, and the Party, in particular, it is necessary that the Party in some way channel these energies into acceptable outlets. One of these is Hate Week. As long as a country is at war, its citizens will put up with personal deprivation. But, the citizens must think that it is a just war, that the enemies are devils whom they are morally obliged to exterminate. The psychology behind Hate Week is precisely that of working up both Party members and proles into a frenzy of self-righteous hate for the enemy, pushing out of their minds all thought of the unsatisfactory lives that they themselves are living.

The Book, which Winston finally is able to read, is Orwell's parody of Leon Trotsky's *The Revolution Betrayed*. Supposedly written by Emmanuel Goldstein, Oceania's official scapegoat — although Winston learns later that O'Brien himself is responsible for it — it is a means by which Oceania can be revealed, as it were, from both the outside and the inside. It is also used, of course, as additional evidence of Winston's need for retraining.

He reads only parts of two chapters. In these, the rise of Oceania and its relationships to Eurasia and Eastasia are described. More important to Winston, perhaps, is the explanation of the means by which the Inner Party keeps power and the way it creates reality. Ingsoc, the Party's official and expedient ideology, is based on a kind of idealism or, as O'Brien readily admits to Winston later, solipsism (a completely enclosed system). Reality is what the Party decides it will be; with power over recorded history, that reality can be, and is, altered day by day. It is largely by this means that the Party controls the minds of its citizens. This alteration is necessary for two reasons. The Party member must have no standard to which he can compare the present. If he is allowed to see that at some time in the past things have been better, then he is potentially dangerous. Second, it is necessary that the Party never be wrong, for a confession of error is a confession of weakness.

All of these mental gymnastics are possible because every Party member, both Inner and Outer, is made proficient in doublethink, the reconciliation of irreconcilable opposites. It is the ability to tell deliberate lies while genuinely believing in them. Characteristically, it is the Inner Party members, who theoretically know that what they are doing and saying is false, who most fervently believe these lies. Thus it is possible to call the torture chambers of the Thought Police the Ministry of Love and to refer to the war department as the Ministry of Peace.

Winston is rather disappointed, in that the book tells him nothing that he does not already know; it merely systematizes what he had thought out in isolated bits. He is happy to learn, however, that he is not insane, that there have been others who have asked the same questions as he and who have been dissatisfied with Ingsoc.

But, having read some of *The Book*, Winston understands only the Party's means, not its end. The answer to that mystery comes from O'Brien in the Ministry of Love, in Part III.

Notes
debauch: an orgy of indulgence in food, drink or sex.
feral: wolflike.
lymph: a colorless bodily fluid.
fecundity: fruitfulness, ability to reproduce.
empirical: a philosophic position in which only observable facts
    are taken into account.

logistics: the study of supplying food and other necessities, and the allocation of quarters; usually refers to an army.
totalitarian: a government that does not allow any opposition to itself. The individual is the absolute servant of the state.
analogies: comparisons.

CHAPTER 10

Summary
Winston and Julia awake from a peaceful sleep and, while they are talking, a voice issues from behind the picture on the wall. The harsh voice from the hidden telescreen instructs Winston and Julia not to move, and they are soon rushed by armed guards. The Thought Police had been observing them all along. Winston and Julia are violently separated. Mr. Charrington enters the room without his disguise, looking much younger. He is a member of the Thought Police.

Commentary
The scene of the arrest of Winston and Julia is rather melodramatic. A scene of domesticity is suddenly transformed into an arena of brutality. Winston acts like a man who has all along expected just this scene, perhaps rehearsed it in his dreams. He is more a product of Oceania than he is ever able to realize and seems almost relieved to have it over with.

With the arrest of Winston and Julia, the thought and the act — the thoughtcrime — have come to the only conclusion possible in such a closed political system. The consequences are all that remain, the punishment, although Winston is to learn to his surprise that it is not immediate death. Julia will virtually disappear from the story; the last act is to be played out between Winston and O'Brien.

In the scene of the arrest, the symbols mentioned earlier figure prominently. The glass paperweight is smashed by the Thought Police. Behind the print of St. Clement's is a telescreen. The nursery rhyme about the bells of the London churches becomes ominous, especially the last line, when repeated by Mr. Charrington. The paperweight especially is reminiscent of an earlier symbol, the Golden Country, about which Winston dreamed before meeting Julia and seeing his dream become reality. The world which he imagined as existing in the paperweight has vanished now as surely as the world of his dream. The single reminder of a past beauty has been smashed.

PART III · CHAPTER 1

Summary

Winston is being held prisoner in a large, crowded cell at the Ministry of Love. Ampleforth and Parsons are both prisoners also. Parsons had been denounced by his own daughter for thoughtcrime. Winston feels increasing physical discomfort. Room 101 is mentioned ominously by several prisoners. O'Brien enters the cell with a guard, and Winston understands that he has been deceived by him. O'Brien is really a member of the Inner Party. O'Brien orders the guard to strike Winston, who feels excruciating pain from the resulting blow to his elbow.

Commentary

Thus, the inevitable, known not only by Winston, but by the reader as well from the very first moments of the story, has come about. Winston is in the hands of the Thought Police, and pain, suffering and confession are no longer inevitable but about to begin. The brutality of the prison is made vivid, as well as its sadistic efficiency. This and following chapters demonstrate brainwashing techniques refined to the ultimate through the use of science in a society gone mad, at least from the point of view of Winston and the reader.

Winston has often remarked that if there is hope, it lies in the proles. This is borne out in the respective attitudes of the Party and the prole prisoners to their imprisonment. The Party members, even Winston, accept their fate without struggle. The proles, on the other hand, fight back, even when they know it is useless. The Party members have been conditioned to react passively; the proles have not.

Winston, essentially a self-centered man, has scarcely any thought of Julia. He knows that he has loved her, and he knows that he will not betray her; but he hardly thinks of her, and there is no particular feeling of love for her now.

Winston realizes now the significance of the phrase which he first heard O'Brien say in a dream, and which O'Brien then echoed in person. In the tiled white rooms of the Ministry of Love, there is no darkness.

Winston is confused about time. He cannot tell daylight from dark since the Ministry building has no windows, and he is unable to calculate with any certainty at all the amount of time that passes. This lack of any ability to mark the passage of time in a meaningful way is part of the way in which the Thought Police disorient the minds of the prisoners. Not being able to calculate the passage of time makes Winston feel emotionally, as well as physically, helpless.

The sense of place, just as the sense of time, has been effectively destroyed. Winston is unable, no matter how hard he tries, to obtain even a hint about his present location. He knows that he must be in the Ministry of Love, but the relative location of the cell in the building is a mystery. This disorientation is another element causing his sense of helplessness.

The fat, sweaty Parsons is the last person that Winston would have expected to commit a thoughtcrime. Parsons' attitude toward his arrest shows the effectiveness of the Party's indoctrination on the majority of its members. Parsons is grateful that he has been arrested and hopes that the Thought Police will be able to root out his evil thoughts about Big Brother and make him a good Party member again. He is actually proud that his young daughter turned him in, proud that she has learned the right things in her training and hopeful that she discovered his thoughtcrime in time to cure it.

The nature of the tortures in Room 101 have been left purposely vague, leaving it to each prisoner to imagine his own worst torture. Since the Thought Police are effective in gathering information from the mind of each Party member, they are actually able to furnish Room 101 with the most horrible torture imaginable to each one personally.

Only six thoughts recur in Winston's brain. He has not been fed since his arrest, and the first two thoughts are caused by hunger. Winston is naturally squeamish; he cannot stand physical pain. He therefore broods on the blood and the screaming. He thinks of Julia, but only in a detached way. O'Brien and the razor blade are connected. Winston has no hope that O'Brien can save him, but there is the hope that O'Brien can smuggle a razor blade in to him so that he can commit suicide before he can be tortured.

Although he consciously dreads physical pain, Winston exhibits an unconscious desire to be punished. If this were not so, he would not have confided in O'Brien, since he here confesses that he has always known O'Brien's true nature. The relationship of Winston toward O'Brien is always shown as that of a son toward his father. Winston thinks that it is O'Brien's strength that he needs to hold him up; in fact, it is O'Brien's chastisement of him that he really desires. He wishes to be punished, first of all, for the way he treated his mother and his little sister. O'Brien, as a father substitute, is the one to do the punishing. Winston has been so molded by the conditioning of the Party that even when he rebels against it, he wishes to be punished by it for that rebellion. O'Brien, an efficient member of the Inner Party, is the perfect instrument to perform the punishment.

This paradox in Winston's mind adds depth to him as a character. He is not the perfect rebel, a type character; he is a man like real men, torn by contrasting elements in his emotional and mental makeup.

CHAPTER 2

Summary

Winston has been tortured physically and mentally for an unknown length of time. His interrogation continues with excessive beatings and questionings until he confesses to a great many crimes of a ridiculous and imaginary nature.

O'Brien directs the questioning and reveals that he has been observing Winston for seven years. O'Brien intends to achieve a complete rehabilitation of Winston. Winston is asked to agree that two plus two equals five and is tortured when he will not do so.

O'Brien explains why there can be no opposition to the Party, and allows Winston to question him. He is informed that Julia quite easily betrayed him, and has now been released, totally rehabilitated. Winston's question about Room 101 is not answered.

Commentary

The police are not able to get inside Winston's head, and he still knows as he confesses that the confessions are lies. The Party intellectuals try to draw him into pitfalls of logic, distort what he says and cause him to doubt his rationality. O'Brien causes Winston to abandon belief in his own sanity. By the use of one of the machines, O'Brien is able to cause Winston's brain to empty completely and, for a short time, Winston is able to believe what O'Brien wishes him to believe, that four fingers are five.

Winston is convinced that, somewhere behind the scenes, O'Brien is directing what is done to him. Winston learns that O'Brien has been watching him for seven years, that it was O'Brien who implanted the dream and the phrase long years before. Winston becomes convinced that O'Brien's mind is so powerful that it contains all of Winston's within it, and more besides. When Winston is reduced to *wanting* to believe what O'Brien says he should believe, the latter rewards him. Because only O'Brien can stop the pain, Winston comes to love him more than ever before, forgetting that O'Brien is also the source of the pain. In the end, Winston becomes convinced of his own insanity and looks to O'Brien for salvation.

Although O'Brien is the torturer, Winston regards him as his friend. He thinks of the pain as an outside thing and the relief from pain as coming from O'Brien. In Winston's mind, the two men are intimates; they can talk together because O'Brien can understand Winston. Although O'Brien tortures him and eventually will order his death, Winston senses the same similarity of mind and temperament O'Brien himself comments on.

That a victim should come to love his torturer is part of the process of conversion. It is also — O'Brien points this out to Winston — a refinement on brainwashing techniques as practised in contemporary totalitarian societies. The conversion must be so total that the victim will thank his tormentors for having converted him and beg to be killed while he is still in a state of grace. And, the victim must regard his own death as a benefit, not to himself because it brings an end to pain, but to the Party because it is the destruction of an unworthy individual. The erring citizen — Winston — must be reborn, only to be destroyed; Orwell constructs here a cruel parody of Christian resurrection.

The Party, to keep functioning, must remain in complete control of the minds of its members, not just control their public actions. When Winston confesses to crimes against the State, the Party sees the confession as true, because Winston has *thought* those crimes, even if he has not been able to commit them.

O'Brien explains to Winston that the Party treats its heretics differently from the way any other authoritarian power has ever used. The Catholic Church, during the period of the Inquisition, destroyed its heretics, but did so while they were unrepentant, making martyrs of them. The totalitarian states of Nazi Germany and Communist Russia forced their heretics to repent, but these men still went to their deaths thinking their heretical thoughts. The Party, however, is deeply concerned with wiping out entirely all heretical thought, so that its deviates go to their deaths sincerely believing that what they have done is wrong. A heretical thought cannot be allowed to exist in the mind of any man, whether he is capable of uttering it or not. His mind must be washed clean before it is destroyed by death. This is absolute power.

Since the Party views any deviation from its line as insanity rather than as crime, the office of the Ministry of Love is to "cure" rather than to punish. The fact that physical and mental torture is used in the cure is of no matter.

Notes
prevaricate: to lie.
ampoule: a single-dose drug container, usually of glass.

CHAPTER 3

Summary
O'Brien tells Winston the second stage of his rehabilitation is about to begin — understanding the "why" of the Party. He also tells Winston that he himself helped write sections of the book supposedly written by Goldstein.

O'Brien goes on to explain that the Party rules for the sake of power, and power alone. The proles will never revolt. In order to re-educate Winston, O'Brien questions him further, and tortures him when he does not answer correctly.

Winston makes a claim to be morally superior to the Party, but O'Brien plays a tape of their conversation about what Winston was willing to do in order to join the Brotherhood. To Winston's claim that the Party will somehow be defeated by something innately noble in man, O'Brien forces Winston to look at his horribly aged and ghastly body in the mirror. Humiliated, Winston weeps, but comforts himself by asserting to O'Brien that despite everything else, he has never betrayed Julia in his heart.

Commentary

Until his arrest and, even for a time afterward, Winston has looked to O'Brien for sanity and strength and kindliness. He now begins to see the older man for what he is — a power-mad fanatic who enjoys the infliction of pain. O'Brien reveals that he is completely skilled in doublethink (all Inner Party members have to be) and is actually able to believe wholeheartedly both the truth and a lie about any subject.

O'Brien has personally watched Winston Smith's development for at least seven years. Winston is puzzled that the Party should expend so much effort on his behalf. O'Brien explains that no amount of effort is spared to root out even one heretical thought from the most lowly of Outer Party members. Absolute power (the goal of the Party) is possible only when there is absolute control over the least member in the organism. O'Brien also adds that Winston's particular type of "insanity" appealed to him intellectually, and he relished the job of "curing" him.

The Party has found that the only way to express absolute power is to inflict pain. The ability to cause suffering is the only concrete way of showing power. It stands to reason, therefore, that the Party is powerful only so long as it inflicts pain upon others. This concept explains many things: the necessity for constant war, the subjection of the proles and the very existence of the Ministry of Love.

The Party, as expressed in O'Brien's comments to Winston, also believes in a simplified idealism. What it desires to be true, what it is expedient to believe as true, *is* true. O'Brien presents this idea of reality in such a way that Winston finds it hard to believe, except that O'Brien is in the position to force him to by means of torture. This view of reality is closely connected with the idea of the alternate past and the control of historical records.

In the philosophy of the Party, the individual man (the man with a "spirit") cannot be allowed to exist. Only the collective man, the man who is able to merge completely with the organism (the Party), surrendering his personal fate to it, can be allowed to live. The Party, working through the person of O'Brien, has effectively destroyed the "spirit" in Winston and, in that sense, Winston is the last man — the last of the old order of men. His kind is doomed to extinction.

Even after being broken in body, mind and spirit, Winston is still able to find satisfaction in the fact that he has not turned against Julia. O'Brien admits that Winston's "reintegration" will not be complete, the Party's mastery will not be total, until Winston does betray Julia. O'Brien is patient, however; he knows that this betrayal must eventually come.

Notes
oligarchy: a country whose government consists of a small, elite group of people.
hedonist: someone who believes that pleasure for its own sake is the highest good.
malleable: changeable.

CHAPTER 4

Summary
Winston's health is improving, and he is trying to accept the rightness of the Party. He examines past events and sees how the Party has been in control of his situation all along. He has been convinced that anything can be true according to the Party's wish and knows that he must re-educate himself to accept the doctrine of the Party and resist argument and disbelief. In other words, that he must practise doublethink.

He wakes up from a troubled sleep calling Julia's name and, soon afterward, O'Brien enters his room. Winston confesses that he still hates Big Brother. O'Brien sends him to Room 101.

Commentary
The key phrase in the chapter is "He accepted everything." Intellectually, Winston does accept everything. O'Brien has successfully emptied out Winston's brain and refurnished it with orthodoxy. Only Winston's love for Julia and hatred for Big Brother stand in the way of complete reintegration.

His dreams are a clue to his continued emotional rebellion. He cannot be considered cured by the Party as long as he clings to the Golden Country. That fantasy must be wiped out.

Strangely enough, Winston does not change very much in his attitude toward O'Brien. Even though the older man has been responsible for the torture he has undergone, Winston still loves him and looks on him as a friend and father. By this point, Winston readily accepts O'Brien's assertion that the torture has been for his own good, that it was necessary to cure him of his insanity; in a sense, he is grateful to O'Brien for inflicting it.

Ironically, O'Brien's job is not complete until he has wiped out Winston's emotional attachment to him. The only creature that Winston may love is Big Brother.

To stop the pain, Winston has surrendered to the Party. With that surrender has come proficiency in doublethink and crimestop. He unconsciously is drawn to write contradictions and slogans on his slate, and he actually accepts and believes them. He now finds, too, that when a dangerous thought is about to intrude, his unconscious mind blocks it out — crimestop has become instinctive.

Throughout the book, it has been tempting to see Winston's rebellion as an intellectual rebellion. It has been less intellectual, however, than emotional. He is broken down intellectually without the necessity for Room 101. His emotional rebellion is more durable. The only way it can be removed is through the supreme torture of that most dreaded chamber in the Ministry of Love.

CHAPTER 5

Summary

In the bright light of the torture room, Room 101, O'Brien informs Winston that the room contains "the worst thing in the world." For Winston, this turns out to be rats in a cage which can be strapped over his face. The rats can then be released in order to attack his face. Winston is totally overcome with horror and terror. He screams that this punishment should be given to Julia instead of him. O'Brien spares him.

Commentary

This very brief chapter is important in identifying the extreme torture. In its terrible efficiency, the Party is able to discover the personal nightmare of each of its members and is able to confront each man with his own. It is the ultimate in personalized torture.

Throughout the novel, Orwell has given clues as to Winston's most dreaded memory, that of the huge carnivorous rats which inhabit the poorer sections of London. The rats that O'Brien uses to move Winston past learning and understanding toward acceptance and love symbolize all that he fears most. Earlier in the novel, with Julia in the room above Mr. Charrington's shop, Winston had been horrified by rats.

Not only does Winston betray Julia, he also betrays that intangible bit of human dignity that he once saw as the salvation of mankind. When he casts off his last element of humanity, he belongs entirely — physically, intellectually and emotionally — to the Party.

Notes
baize: a type of cloth.
impalement: penetration by a wooden stake.
rats: This recalls Winston's expressed fear of rats in Part II, Chapter 4.
didactically: as though trying to instruct or teach someone.

CHAPTER 6
Summary
Winston has been released and is sitting in the Chestnut Tree Café. He drinks very heavily now. He remembers meeting Julia, and their conversation about having betrayed each other. Though the Party would now allow them to continue their relationship, neither one feels anything for the other. He begins to remember a pleasant game of his childhood, but pushes it out of his mind when a political broadcast comes on the telescreen. Eurasia is once again the enemy. His heart fills with love for Big Brother.

Commentary
There is a religious character to this last chapter, as well as a political one. The Party is Power, and God is Power. The Party, in the person of Big Brother, is God.

The Chestnut Tree Café is an appropriate setting for the last chapter of *1984*. It was in this bar that Winston saw Jones, Aaronson and Rutherford after their fall from grace. Just as the other patrons of the bar avoided the trio, they now avoid Winston. The song associated with the bar now has personal meaning for Winston, since he has betrayed Julia.

The final, and inevitable change takes place at this final moment; Winston is healed. He demonstrates his sanity by being able to express his love of Big Brother. This is the ultimate surrender, the surrender of feelings. It is the complete triumph of the Party over the individual and the total destruction of the spirit of man.

Thus, in a period covering approximately one calendar year, Winston has gone through the entire cycle. Just about a year earlier, he had his initial contact with Julia. They spent about four months together, and then he was in the Ministry of Love for about nine months, like a child in the womb.

Notes

Chestnut Tree Café: Winston now frequents the same bar as Jones, Aaronson and Rutherford had, after their defeat and rehabilitation.

It was a false memory: Winston is able to think this now because he has succeeded at doublethink.

APPENDIX: THE PRINCIPLES OF NEWSPEAK

Summary

The aim of Newspeak is to reduce the number of words in the language. The theory underlying this is that if there are fewer words, then there will be less opportunity to think. If the people cannot think except within an increasingly small range, then they will not question or criticize the government. Also, the simpler the language in both rules and actual number of words, the easier it will be for the proles to learn it. The basic, simplified language will be useful in uniting all the citizens at a very fundamental level.

If ambiguity and all subtleties of language are removed, then imagination will eventually disappear. With the disappearance of imagination will come the disappearance of anyone's ability to imagine a system or government other than the one that exists.

Commentary

The language which Orwell devised as the official language of Oceania — Newspeak — is an extension of what he saw happening in the use of English in his own time: lying and deceit for political purposes. Orwell believed that careless use of language corrupted thought and that inexact thinking had a bad effect on language. For his society of the future, he conceived of a language whose purpose was wholly political, not communicative. Newspeak is another, and powerful, means by which the Party retains its hold over its citizens by making unorthodox thoughts impossible. If there are no words for unacceptable ideas or thoughts, they will cease to exist or to be a threat to those in power. Orwell projects this use of language to its ultimate end: the complete silencing of speech and, therefore, thought. The ideal response for the sake of orthodoxy is inarticulate noise, or "duckspeak."

Orwell's creation of the new language is ingenious: for instance, he uses the present characteristic of the language called functional shift (the tendency of words to move easily from one part of speech to another). He also gives examples of the use of Newspeak during the course of the story. One which reveals especially well what Newspeak is like is the order to Winston in Newspeak — which is translated into "Oldspeak" or Standard English — to revise a speech of Big Brother's.

Notes
staccato: sharp, detached.
ipso facto: by that very fact; a proof or demonstration.
euphemisms: mild terms substituted for violent, harsh realities.
inimical: hostile.
panegyric: a praising song or verse.

Character Sketches

Winston Smith

Winston is both a character in his own right and a representative of an idea. In the society of Oceania — a society of the future which Orwell envisioned as a comment on the present — Winston is an anachronism. His mind and personality are not at first defined by the Party slogans, by the Party's ideas of what he should be. From his own point of view, he is an individual; from the Party's point of view, he is a flaw in the reality it is creating.

Winston might be thought of as an instance of the modern hero, as opposed to the older or Aristotelian tragic hero. The modern hero, often an ordinary man, is destroyed by the society of which he is a part. To put it differently, society deprives itself of one of its members, and herein lies the tragedy, if that is what it is to be called. The society of Oceania, however, survives to carry out its purposes only by destroying those who do not conform to its notion of reality. To maintain that world requires assent at every level from its citizens.

During the course of the novel Winston changes — from a man who is vaguely out of place in Oceania, who is annoyed by the limits placed on his individuality — to a man who has been made to conform to the world the Party has created. From our point of view, the change in Winston is for the worse; for the Party, it is for the better, and necessary.

In his person, Winston is, above all, ordinary, although his intelligence is above average. In any other society, Orwell seems to imply, he would go unnoticed. But, in Oceania, the fact that he wants to feel human, to sense his individuality makes him extraordinary; to O'Brien and the Party it makes him a man to watch and, finally, to rehabilitate. Winston surprises himself at his daring, although he is unable to act until someone else — Julia, O'Brien — initiates the move. But, from the first, he expects defeat of whatever form his rebellion takes, whether keeping a diary or entering into a liaison with Julia. He knows too well, even as he realizes he loves Julia, that there really is no hope.

Julia

As a young woman whose view of life is a simple one — contentment consists of real chocolate, a double bed to sleep in and casual sexual experiences — Julia is used by Orwell as both a means and a foil. It is by means of the liaison with her that Winston makes his public break with society and acts out his thoughtcrime, which has characterized his state of mind from the beginning. Julia is also a foil, in her simple view of life, to the reason Winston rebels. Although at first it is dissatisfaction with the quality of his daily life, plus nostalgia for the past, that causes him to act against his own well-being and safety, it is finally a matter of principle with Winston.

Like Winston, however, Julia is also a believable person. She is an earth-goddess figure, in a sense, because she responds, not thinks. Winston's reading of *The Book*, for instance, puts her to sleep. The only thinking she does is with her body and her feelings. She tries to reach Winston in this way, but he is not content to oppose society solely because it bores him but must find a reason for doing so. Julia is a rebel, under cover of outward conformity, only because Oceania fails to satisfy her need for companionship and sexual fulfilment.

O'Brien

O'Brien is almost the only member of the Inner Party to appear as a character in the novel. He represents the ruling oligarchy, but more than that he *is* the Party for Winston Smith. As Winston discovers during the nine months spent with O'Brien in the Ministry of Love, the official is the embodiment in daily life of the symbol of Big Brother. It is clear enough in the novel that Big Brother is only a symbol for display, not an individual. But O'Brien, putting Winston through physical and psychological torture, is very much an individual, very much alive, and thus someone to whom Winston can and does relate.

O'Brien shows a certain kind of intelligence in his long conversations with Winston: the kind that is capable of, or has adapted to, believing anything. It is perhaps great mental agility and thorough training that O'Brien has, rather than what is usually called intelligence. To Winston, he makes a virtue, as the Party does, of thinking and not thinking (acceptance), what in Newspeak is designated doublethink. He also emphasizes, in Winston's education for conformity, that reality is what Big Brother or the Party decides it is. He offers himself as a living example of one who lives, not merely accepts these basic principles.

The human qualities he shows to Winston — making himself appear to be a friend, confidant, confessor, teacher — are ruthlessly assumed for the job he has been assigned to do: make Winston acceptable to the Party and, at the same time, harmless. Having no other choice, Winston must take these qualities at face value. O'Brien plays his role well: at the end of the novel, Winston easily transfers his affection for O'Brien to Big Brother. After all, O'Brien exists only if and as Big Brother, the Party, wishes him to exist.

Literary Elements

Meaning and Structure

1984 is not a prophecy of the future, but rather a criticism of existing trends of which Orwell wished to warn his readers. The major trend being satirized is the amoral pursuit of power which results in fear and violence. Both fear and violence become tools of this pursuit of power. The quest for power can be described as amoral because every value and quality of life, even language, is judged only in terms of its usefulness to obtaining, keeping and extending power. This approach to power becomes clear in *1984*, and Orwell is careful to paint an exact picture of what the effects of this attitude are in the fictional world of Oceania. By presenting this picture of exaggerated trends of the contemporary world, Orwell's objective is to urge improvement of society. He wished his readers to gain an awareness of the possible results of neglecting to do so. The result, in Orwell's opinion, of failing to solve the problem of power-madness is clearly specified in O'Brien's picture of the future: "imagine a boot stamping on a human face — forever."

The structure of society in *1984* is outlined in a fictional political document, *The Theory and Practice of Oligarchal Collectivism*, which is read by the main character just prior to his arrest and spiritual destruction by the Party. The Party itself is seeking absolute power for the sake of power, and everything is sacrificed to that end. The basis for the Party's rule is that of the lie. History is changed to conform with policy, the language itself is being transformed in order to make the population easier to manipulate. Big Brother, the terrifying paternal leader figure, and Goldstein, the archenemy of the Party, are both manufactured by the Party in order to manipulate Oceania's citizens, as well. The slogans chosen by the Party, upon which the theory of government rests, are typical of the falsity and hypocrisy of their reign of terror: WAR IS PEACE, FREEDOM IS SLAVERY and IGNORANCE IS STRENGTH. The practice of doublethink and Newspeak is the institutionalization of falsehood on a systematic basis. The totalitarian government of the Party has its own secret police, the Thought Police, and privacy has been done away with through two-way telescreens and strict regimentation of all activity and use of leisure time. Poverty and eternal warfare (or the impression thereof) are additional tools which are used to keep the population in line.

The plot of the novel involves the rebellion and defeat of Winston Smith. His individualism must be destroyed completely, because the Party allows no exceptions. Winston must not only be defeated, but must be transformed into a willing slave of the Party's policies. Because of the Party's hunger for power, he is not allowed to even remain master of his own soul or mind. The all-consuming hunger for power admits no barriers, and must have complete dominion over everything.

The plot structure develops in terms of Winston's decline, fall and salvation from rebellion against the Party. The notion of his spiritual destruction at the hands of the Party as a form of salvation is an indication of the perverse, upside down system produced by the quest for absolute power, in which nothing is safe, and even meaning itself is in danger.

Theme

The theme of the novel can be viewed in two ways or consists of two sides of the same idea. For Winston Smith, life consists of physical love, physical pain and psychological destruction (or change). For the society of Oceania, life consists of power. As O'Brien points out to Winston in the Ministry of Love, "... the Party seeks power for its own sake.... Power is not a means; it is an end." To maintain power, the Party must rehabilitate Winston Smith, through pain, and then destroy him when he has been rendered harmless.

In the way in which he views himself in relation to the Party, in the way in which he attempts to defend himself, or rather his view of life, in the encounter with O'Brien in the Ministry of Love, Winston is indeed "the last man." There are several possible synonymous expressions for O'Brien's contemptuous label: the last liberal, the last humanist. Whatever the expression, Winston is an anachronism in Oceania, at least from the Party's point of view, because of the value he places upon the individual. Yet, it is, of course, the individual that he is finally made to betray: himself, Julia. Winston is unable to resist anywhere — in mind, or heart or spirit — the Party's draining out of his individuality and replacing it with itself. There is no I, only we, only Big Brother.

To think, instead of to accept, is automatic nonconformity and treason in Oceania. The Party slogans indicate this, and certainly this is the aim of Newspeak. Oceania's official language is designed to produce conformity without thought, to make thoughtcrime impossible. In short, it is to make impossible the occurrence of another Winston Smith.

Several critics have pointed out the way in which the proles, in Orwell's imaginary society, are left almost untouched by the relentless pressures for conformity. The Party's official view is that no leaders will ever arise from such a source and, therefore, no threat to order is possible. It is true, however, that in totalitarian societies as we know them no class of people is left untouched by the central government.

Ingsoc, Newspeak for English Socialism, is the official rationalization of the Party's sole aim of power. The choice of name for the Party's ideology is, in part, an indication of the sources for Orwell's society of Oceania. Most critics see this society as combining features not only of England, especially in wartime (World War II), but also of Russia and, perhaps, of the Germany of Hitler's era.

The other means by which the Party maintains power are, of course, justified in the doctrines of Ingsoc: its view of the past and consequent daily rewriting of history; its complete subjugation of the citizens of Oceania by, for example, rechanneling sexual desire; its maintaining of a perpetual state of warfare — or illusion of such a state — with the other two world powers; its use of a scapegoat (Emmanuel Goldstein) and its simplified mind-over-matter idealism.

1984 is also an attempt by Orwell to awaken us to a very real danger which he perceived. The danger is that man could actually be transformed into an unfeeling machine. Orwell saw trends of barbarism and the absolutely amoral quest for power in his own time. He could not accept the optimistic belief that the state of the world improves with every technological advance. He saw the rise of totalitarianism, but he was just as disturbed by what he believed was the readiness of liberal Western governments to adopt the same methods of oppression and brutality as the fascists and communists, in fighting those ideologies. What Orwell hoped to illustrate in his novel is that, if these tendencies toward militarism, brutality and dehumanization continue, the fictional world of *1984* could easily become a reality.

Style

The style of *1984* resembles that of journalism in its direct and simple presentation. Many sections begin with very short, simple sentences which immediately introduce the reader to a situation, or summing up previous action in a concise manner: for example, "Syme had vanished" (Part II, Chapter 5), or "It had happened at last" (Part II, Chapter 6). Other typical stylistic characteristics include the repetition of certain sentence structures and the use of lists. These lists are most often the piling up of details in descriptions, such as the description of the prole woman in Part II, Chapter 9. Many other examples can be found (i.e., Part III, Chapter 2). Repetitive sentence structure is used for emphasis and effect, such as in the repeated use of "It was he . . ." to describe O'Brien in Part III, Chapter 2, and the use of "they" to open five consecutive sentences in Part III, Chapter 4.

These stylistic devices are extremely effective in the reinforcement of a mood of stark monotony. In this, they are particularly suited to the impression which Orwell wished to convey, of a society of enforced conformity and denial of free will. There is a harmony between Orwell's style and the principles of Newspeak, which he introduces.

Diction, Emphasis and Imagery

The essence of George Orwell's style is his crisp, sharp diction. In *1984*, Orwell uses a journalistic technique of description. He describes Oceania, and life there, in a clear and economical manner. He does not waste words and uses a straightforward, easily understood vocabulary. By and large, his sentence structure is simple and to the point. Most critics agree that Orwell's greatest asset as a craftsman was his ability to cut through emotions with simple, precise language without unnecessary flourishes. Some critics have complained, however, of his lack of an individualized diction and of his occasional choppy sentences.

The emphasis of the novel is exceptionally well handled. The time Orwell spends on details may seem excessive at first. However, Orwell carefully connects these particular details and subordinates them to larger ideas. The adeptness with which Orwell treats emphasis in *1984* is a result of both his peculiar talent and the time and care he expended on his final work.

The imagery of *1984* is also the result of great care. It is similar to the diction in that it is clear and precise. Probably the most famous descriptive line in the novel is found in Goldstein's discussion of the three superstates cooperating with one another in the perpetual war. This and the many other examples (such as the "boot stamping on a human face . . . forever.") are illustrative of Orwell's fondness for exact, concrete similes. The dominant imagery throughout the novel is connected with decay and filth. This, along with the dreary, colorless mood such imagery evokes, is used in brilliant contrast to the Golden Country, the light, bright place of beauty and freedom.

Orwell's style is simple and, to a large extent, colloquial. His is not an individualized style. His precision, attention to detail and ability to formulate the exact image to embody the larger idea make him an expert craftsman and a distinguished stylist.

Point of View

Every work of literature is told or recorded by someone, but usually the artist either assumes a *persona* (masking himself as a character within the work) or removes himself from that work. *1984* is told from the third person point of view. That is, Orwell is not himself a character in the book. The recorder of the story is omniscient and removed from involvement in the plot. Point of view also includes the attitude of the narrator toward the story he tells. For example, in *1984*, we are concerned with whether the narrator approves or disapproves of the events that take place within the context of the book. Of course, in this work, the narrator expresses neither approval nor disapproval in any direct comments to the reader. That is, he is a neutral narrator — he merely records the story. The student should not confuse the narrator's disinterestedness with the author's. By his choice of details, Orwell expresses his disapproval of Oceanic society. That disapproval is implicit, however, never explicit and "preachy."

Symbols

Orwell's use of symbols is both careful and restrained. Symbols such as the ever-present dust, Winston's ulcer, the glass paperweight and the nursery rhymes are woven into the fabric of the novel. It is not always possible to give a single meaning to any of these symbols, because they often suggest more than one thing at a time.

The prevalence of references to dust, erosion and decay in the novel convey both a sense of bleak foreboding, and an impression that the quality of life in Oceania is being constantly eroded and degraded by the machinery of government. The novel opens with "a swirl of gritty dust," and Mrs. Parsons looks as if there were dust in the creases of her face. Winston closes his diary and places a piece of dust on the cover to tell if it has been opened. Thus, from the very outset, the reader is given a subtle indication that the world of the novel is not a pleasant, nor a pretty, one. Later, Julia and Winston make love on a dusty floor, and in a bomb blast, they are both covered in dust. Dust, then, as a symbol, pervades the book. It is both complete in itself, and implies something other, and larger, than itself.

The glass paperweight, which Winston buys in the antique shop, symbolizes the enduring past, which is tied to Winston's hope for a better life, in which there can be such qualities as truth and beauty. In itself, it is a significant link with the past that is being erased, and yet trivial because it is a small and non-functional item. It is representative of what Winston believes the Party cannot destroy, and comes to symbolize both Winston's dream of happiness and that part of him which he thinks the Party cannot touch. Having come to represent such things, the destruction of the paperweight by the Thought Police predicts Winston's eventual destruction, and increases the reader's sense of foreboding.

The nursery rhymes also have a nostalgic value, like the paperweight. They, however, have become distorted and manipulated by the Party, until one such rhyme ends with the "I sold you and you sold me" variation so expressive of certain later events in the novel. Its former affirmation of family life and love has become twisted by the Party. Winston's quest for the final lines of the rhyme "Oranges and Lemons" represent, in a minor way, his quest for some better kind of life. The perversely twisted ending of the rhyme illustrates the fate of Winston in his quest.

Doublethink and Newspeak

Doublethink is basically a schizophrenic way of thinking in contradictory terms at the same time. It is enforced by the Party in order to deny citizens of Oceania any possibility of questioning rapid and hypocritical changes in policy. Thus, it is both an effective and terrifying tool of government. It indicates the ability of the Party to control minds and thoughts.

Orwell named the process, but by no means did he invent it. He had observed, in his time, the process by which a totalitarian state reversed its policies and demanded unswerving loyalty, even in the face of wild variations. At one stage of World War II, the Soviet Union was allied with Hitler, and then suddenly he was declared an enemy. In *1984*, doublethink indicates the corruption of mind enforced by a totalitarian state, the attitude which maintains orthodoxy and loyalty in spite of anything. Those who are most successful at doublethink are the members of the Inner Party.

Newspeak is the tool created and used by the Party to encourage and enforce doublethink. It represents a cheapening and limitation of language, which illustrates the abuse of language for political purposes, that was becoming increasingly prevalent at the time of the novel's composition. The intention of Newspeak is to discard more and more words and meanings until rebellion is not possible because there is no word for it. The underlying principle is that if certain words and meanings are removed from the language, the ideas they represent will soon follow. A restriction and remodelling of the language will increasingly limit each citizen's ability to think for himself. Thus, language itself in *1984* is seen as a tool of government. Newspeak is also a satire on what Orwell saw as the increasing abuse of language for political and commercial purposes in his own time.

The Appendix concerning the principles of Newspeak is an indication of the seriousness of the problem in Orwell's eyes. This section could possibly be seen as a flaw in the artistic integrity of the novel, and it is true that the novel can indeed be read without it since Orwell has dealt with the basic approach of Newspeak in Part I, Chapter 5. However, The Appendix does exist as a valuable elaboration of certain themes in the novel, particularly that of the abuse of power. The concern with the abuse of language was obviously of such concern to Orwell that he considered an elaboration on the tool of doublethink to be necessary. Also, along with the long sections from Goldstein's *The Theory and Practice of Oligarchal Collectivism* which are included in Part II, the Appendix might also possibly be seen as an attempt on Orwell's part to achieve a bleak, theoretical reality for the concepts central to his satiric approach.

It is also interesting as a document and fiction in its own right, and bears a definite relation to certain other works by Orwell, particularly his important essay, "Politics and the English language."

*Orwell's Image of the Man of Good Will

It has often been said, and rightly so, that George Orwell is a political writer; the label, however, can mean many things. Applied to Orwell, it means that from his first book to his last he is concerned with the nature of modern man's life in intimate relationship to the society of which he is a part and for which, in however small a way, he is responsible. But more particularly, it means that Orwell's work is a developing chronicle of the life and times of the man of good will in a world of which he is often uneasily a part and for which he is sometimes unwillingly responsible.

To understand this man moving through this world is, it has often been said, to encounter Orwell's common sense and plain style. To be sure, Orwell's sense is common; his style, plain; certainly to say this is to commend him. However, through the common sense and the plain style arise images which are the creation of a man who sees with both his common sense and his imagination. Surrounded by Orwell's clear look at what is and firmly embedded in his old-fashioned truthfulness, the images lead to a double view of the man of good will: what he means as a representative modern man and how uncomfortably close he is to us.

In his last novel, *1984*, Orwell gives us the image of the man of good will in the near future. Perhaps it would be more exact to say that Orwell presents several images of Winston Smith, the man of the future. Winston is both an uneasy and unwilling citizen of the society of Oceania. Not an intellectual, he is unable to understand why Oceania is the kind of society it is and why the Party acts in the guise it uses and therefore is unable to make his resistance on theoretical grounds. However, because of his feeling that the past was not like the present and because of a succession of fitful recollections of his own past, he believes that something has gone wrong in Oceania.

Because of the nature of Winston's unorthodoxy, it is of some importance to understand the way in which he views himself, his aspirations, and the possible life for himself amid the

*By Frank H. Thompson, Jr. From *College English*, XXII, No. 4 (January, 1961). Reprinted by permission of the National Council of Teachers of English.

telescreens and posters of Oceania. It is in his dreams that we first encounter his private idyllic landscape, "the Golden Country."

> Suddenly he was standing on short springy turf, on a summer evening when the slanting rays of the sun gilded the ground. The landscape that he was looking at recurred so often in his dreams that he was never fully certain whether or not he had seen it in the real world. In his waking thoughts he called it the Golden Country. It was an old, rabbit-bitten pasture, with a foot track wandering across it and a mole-hill here and there. In the ragged hedge on the opposite side of the field the boughs of the elm trees were swaying very faintly in the breeze, their leaves just stirring in dense masses like women's hair. Somewhere near at hand, though out of sight, there was a clear, slow-moving stream where dace were swimming in the pools under the willow trees.
> The girl with dark hair was coming toward him across the field. With what seemed a single movement she tore off her clothes and flung them disdainfully aside. Her body was white and smooth, but it aroused no desire in him; indeed, he barely looked at it. What overwhelmed him in that instant was admiration for the gesture with which she had thrown her clothes aside. With its grace and carelessness it seemed to annihilate a whole culture, a whole system of thought, as though Big Brother and the Party and the Thought Police could all be swept into nothingness by a single splendid movement of the arm. That too was a gesture belonging to the ancient time (pp. 31-32).[1]

And in spite of what knowledge he has of the Party by virtue of his belonging to the Outer Party and his daily awareness in his job of the reality which the Party is systematically fabricating, Winston believes in the dream, in the gesture. He feels it must represent hope for him because, in spite of what he knows, he wants to be hopeful. When, later, he goes with Julia to the country, though he experiences a "shock of recognition" (p. 124) at realizing that they are in the landscape of his dream, in the

66

Golden Country, he feels that it is right that they should be in this place, not elsewhere. This rightness of feeling is reinforced when Julia makes the splendid gesture of the girl with the dark hair. To Winston, the scene signifies the dream or hope becoming the reality. The logic of feeling leads him to think of the sexual act as "a blow struck against the Party. It was a political act" (p. 128). For Winston what happens in this apparently real Golden Country is the next logical step from the heresies written in his diary.

The large image of Winston's hope is the Golden Country; the small is the glass paperweight which he buys from Mr. Charrington. Winston is attracted to the paperweight in the first place because it comes from an older time, from what he calls the ancient time, as does the magnificently careless gesture of the girl with the dark hair who becomes Julia in the present. But, again like the Golden Country, what represents the past becomes Winston's best hope for the present. During the first time he and Julia spend in the room above Mr. Charrington's shop, Winston studies the paperweight.

> The inexhaustibly interesting thing was not the fragment of coral but the interior of the glass itself. There was such a depth of it, and yet it was almost as transparent as air. It was as though the surface of the glass had been the arch of the sky, enclosing a tiny world with its atmosphere complete. He had the feeling that he could get inside it, and that in fact he was inside it, along with the mahogany bed and the gateleg table and the clock and the steel engraving and the paperweight itself. The paperweight was the room he was in, and the coral was Julia's life and his own, fixed in a sort of eternity at the heart of the crystal (p. 148).

As the sexual act with Julia is a blow against the Party, against its extinction of the human emotions and feelings and pleasures, so the vision of his life and Julia's fixed in an inviolate eternity is another, though different, blow against the Party, against its crushing of the private life and therefore private emotions and thought, against the unsleeping, prying eyes of the telescreen and Thought Police. But, it is precisely the Thought Police who smash the paperweight when Winston and Julia are arrested, who smash what seems to Winston to be true and important. The eternity is but an expendable paperweight, and the Golden Country is but a foolish dream.

What has smashed the world of Winston and Julia, a world of hope against hope, is the reality which the Party is continuously creating. And in that reality there are no individuals at all, only the Party, which is epitomized in the stern but yet almost benign face of Big Brother as he is represented on the ubiquitous poster. In his re-education of Winston, O'Brien tries to explain that the Party member is in effect but an appendage of Big Brother, that each member exists only in such a function as the Party decides he will exist. As O'Brien points out to Winston, he no longer exists; he is but an example of unorthodoxy which the Party cannot tolerate and which it will change. Just as Winston is obsessed by images of his hope, so the Party has its obsession with an image of the human being: for an image of the future, O'Brien asks Winston to imagine " 'a boot stamping on a human face — forever' " (p. 271).

Winston, one who does not exist because in the Party's convoluted logic he has chosen not to exist, the Party sees in two striking ways: pictures of before and after. At one point in the process of re-education, O'Brien tells Winston to take off his clothes and look at himself in a triple mirror. Winston has just said to O'Brien that somehow the Party will be defeated by " 'some spirit, some principle' " and when asked what this principle is replies: " 'The spirit of Man' " (p. 273). After telling Winston that if he is a man he is the last man, O'Brien then orders Winston to look at himself, the last man, in the mirror. "A bowed, gray-colored, skeletonlike thing was coming toward him. Its actual appearance was frightening, and not merely the fact that he knew it to be himself " (p. 274). To reinforce Winston's horror and despair at seeing his condition, O'Brien describes in detail what the mirror reveals and then concludes: " 'You are rotting away . . . you are falling to pieces. What are you? A bag of filth. Now turn around and look into that mirror again. Do you see that thing facing you? That is the last man. If you are human, that is humanity' " (p. 275). This is the image of man that the Party has created: a bag of filth. This is the individual before he has lost his identity in the iron discipline of the Party and the omnipotence of Big Brother.

But there is a second image. O'Brien tells Winston that his re-education consists of more than learning and understanding; its final goal is acceptance. The Party, says O'Brien, will drain him and fill him with itself; the change that will inevitably happen in the Ministry of Love will be forever. At this point Winston calculates the concessions he has made and resolves to hold out against the last, the most crucial one: he has conceded outward orthodoxy in order to retain intellectual integrity; then the mind in order to keep the inner heart inviolate; this last he will hold onto till the end. But he has not reckoned on the horror of Room 101, that unspeakable confrontation that literally drives the mind out of the already ruined body. He has been drained and filled with the Party, with Big Brother.

> He gazed up at the enormous face. Forty years it had taken him to learn what kind of smile was hidden beneath the dark mustache. O cruel, needless misunderstanding! O stubborn, self-willed exile from the loving breast! Two gin-scented tears trickled down the sides of his nose. But it was all right, everything was all right, the struggle was finished. He had won the victory over himself. He loved Big Brother (p. 300).

Here is the image of the Party member, or would be if Winston were not eventually to be executed. Here at least is what Winston should have been all along: a mindless bundle of flesh to hate when the Party says to hate, to exult over another victory when the Party declares exultation appropriate, to work ceaselessly and enthusiastically for the Party in whatever way it decides that work is to be done. Here is the image of after to place beside that of before, the bag of filth. These are the alternatives for the Party: a thing that calls itself man or a mindless statistic at one with Big Brother.

The images of man as represented by Winston Smith in *1984* are the last and certainly the most horrifying in Orwell's work. Just as they are plausible and right, so they are the final images in a succession occurring throughout Orwell's novels, political works, and essays. And the last are related to the others in such a way that it has been said earlier that Orwell's work is a developing chronicle of the life of the man of good will in modern times. If the chronicle develops, then the predecessors of Winston Smith can be traced. His spiritual ancestors can be found among the animals of *Animal Farm*, in George Bowling of *Coming Up for Air*, in Gordon Comstock of *Keep the Aspidistra Flying*, in John Flory of *Burmese Days*, in the autobiographical Orwell of *Down and Out in Paris and London* and *Homage to Catalonia*. Of all these prior works, the one most suited for the role of antecedent of *1984* is *Homage to Catalonia*, Orwell's account of the Spanish Civil War. For here in Spain of the 1930's is a classic example of what in our time has become commonplace: the revolution betrayed. Here in a revolution advertised as a civil war Orwell finds images of the man of good will amid treachery and deceit, losing his aspirations to what in the year 1984 has become the Party.

What for Winston Smith in 1984 is hope against hope seems real hope in Barcelona of 1936. Early in the book, Orwell comments: "I mention this Italian militiaman because he has stuck vividly in my memory. With his shabby uniform and fierce pathetic face he typifies for me the special atmosphere of that time" (p. 4).[2] Barcelona is in a strange and wonderful state; the working class does in fact and for the moment rule.

> And it was the aspect of the crowds that was the queerest thing of all. In outward appearance it was a town in which the wealthy classes had practically ceased to exist. Except for a small number of women and foreigners there were no "well-dressed" people at all. Practically everyone wore rough working-class clothes, or blue overalls or some variant of the militia uniform. All this was queer and moving (p. 5).

But the exhilaration of equality is not confined to the citizens of Barcelona; it infects also the party militias, the irregulars who form what seems to Orwell a real people's army.

> One had been in a community where hope was more normal than apathy or cynicism, where the word "comrade" stood for comradeship and not, as in most countries, for humbug. One had breathed the air of equality ... the Spanish militias, while they lasted, were a sort of microcosm of a classless society (pp. 104-105).

And the people of Catalonia act as though the revolution were fact, not possibility. The spirit of the people at this time, according to Orwell's account, is genuine; the hopes, enthusiastic but yet sensible.

Then comes Orwell's return from the front to Barcelona in April, 1937. It is not the same Barcelona of a few months before: ". . . the revolutionary atmosphere had vanished" (p. 109). The change is evident everywhere.

> The change in the aspect of the crowds was startling. The militia uniform and the blue overalls had almost disappeared; everyone seemed to be wearing the smart summer suits in which Spanish tailors specialize. Fat prosperous men, elegant women, and sleek cars were everywhere.

What has happened that the fighting men on the front have not heard about, have had no inkling of? Orwell outlines the changes lucidly: the Communists, supplied with arms and directives from Russia, have decided that the war but not the revolution is to be supported; for reasons of world politics, Russia cannot afford a revolution in Spain and is in a position to see that it is quashed. The inter-party politics on the Republican side is complicated and treacherous.

Power exerts itself quickly. As O'Brien tells Winston, in *1984*, power is power over people, and power is exercised only when people are made to suffer. In Barcelona, power is exercised: the Stalinist wing of the Communist Party takes advantage of the natural inertia of the government. The men of good will of whatever particular political persuasion cannot believe that the Stalinists, having the same general aspirations and ideals as any other party on the Republican side, will turn their advantage into persecution.

> It is not easy to convey the nightmare atmosphere of that time — the peculiar uneasiness produced by rumours that were always changing, by censored newspapers and the constant presence of armed men. It is not easy to convey it because, at the moment, the thing essential to such an atmosphere does not exist in England. In England political intolerance is not yet

taken for granted. There is political persecution in a petty way; if I were a coal-miner I would not care to be known to the boss as a Communist; but the "good party man," the gangster-gramophone of continental politics, is still a rarity, and the notion of "liquidating" or "eliminating" everyone who happens to disagree with you does not yet seem natural. It seemed only too natural in Barcelona. The "Stalinists" were in the saddle, and therefore it was a matter of course that every "Trotskyist" was in danger (p. 198).

The persecutions begin: men of the "wrong" party are jailed; many are held incommunicado; others are executed. Hiding from the secret police of the Stalinists becomes a necessity. Meanwhile, the war with Franco goes on, but the revolution is in the process of being crushed.

In this account of the struggle for power on the Republican side, Orwell gives two images of the well-meaning partisan of the revolution: one, really a composite, is that of the many faces of hope, determination, and good will which appear briefly and never are seen again; the other, an interesting foil to the first, is that of Orwell himself. Being a man capable of genuine candor, Orwell pictures himself as ignorant and unknowing as the next soldier in understanding that the revolution is being betrayed. He admits to the difficulty of not wanting to believe until the last moment that the Stalinists really mean to make the most of the situation; no one wants to believe that they mean to go beyond the intelligent position of agreeing to disagree. No one, and Orwell gives himself as an example, can really understand power and the full impact of its exercise.

But since the time is 1937, not 1984, since the Stalinists are not yet the Party, since the war or the revolution or both are but small affairs (at least, in size), there is time to reflect. Orwell, his own image of the man of good will, has time to reflect and learn as Winston Smith, much later, cannot. Upon reflection, the betrayal of the revolution in Spain can be a lesson but also a prophecy. As to the future of Spain, whoever wins the war, Orwell writes: "But I still believe that — unless Spain splits up, with unpredictable consequences — the tendency of the post-war Government is bound to be Fascistic" (p. 182). The alternatives are a dictatorship of Franco or a dictatorship of a Stalinist or Stalinist-ridden government.

From the reality of the Spanish Civil War to the unreality of Oceania seems a distressingly short step. Perhaps the "unreality" of Oceania arises from the belief on the part of Orwell's man of good will that the betrayal of good intentions and the exercise of power as the power to make men suffer, as shown in a preliminary fashion in Spain and on a wider scale since, must be unreal; it just cannot be so. But in spite of the hope, it seems to; O'Brien's image of " 'a boot stamping on a human face — forever' " seems to be a prediction that is bound to come true, come what may.

The power of Orwell's image of the man of good will comes from his including himself always among the well-intentioned but duped. He is in Spain and must, like others, hide from persecution; he is also in Winston Smith. It is clear that Orwell takes the last step of honesty and includes himself in the figure of what O'Brien calls the last man. In a very meaningful sense, Orwell is Winston Smith, just as other men of common sense and good intentions are Winston Smith. The implication is clear enough: whether we want to be Winston or not, we will be; and to be Winston is to be the last man.

Critics evidently have been troubled by this conclusion. Perhaps if Orwell's death had not been untimely, they say, he might have clarified what he meant in *1984*. But what needs to be clarified? The man of good will is the man of old-fashioned virtues, and Orwell believes in these. But in a world that believes in the new the old-fashioned is but a foolish memory. In 1984 there is nothing old-fashioned because the world is created anew every day: a perpetual Eden turned upside down. But for Orwell, and for his man of sense and hope, what prospect is there? There is no prospect, except that of Winston in the Ministry of Love and Winston adoring Big Brother. And what consolation, then? None, except to recall that Winston does not always love Big Brother, that there is a time before the Ministry of Love.

Notes

[1] George Orwell, *1984* (New York: Harcourt, Brace and Co., 1949). All references in parentheses are to this edition.

[2] George Orwell, *Homage to Catalonia* (Boston: The Beacon Press, 1955). All references in parentheses are to this edition.

Selected Criticisms

Mr. Orwell wastes no time in describing possible gadgets of the new era, nor in being satirical or funny or purely fantastic. His is a rapt concern for the plight of the human race, and in calm prose of high excellence, he directs his diatribes chiefly at Soviet Communism and English Socialism, but also, for the rest of us, living perhaps too smugly under the aegis of Democracy, he sounds a liberal and rational note of warning that we examine our motives and study the meaning of our shibboleths.

M. P. Corcoran. *Catholic World*, Vol. 169 (1949).

... hope has died in Mr. Orwell's wintry mind, and only pain is known. I do not think I have ever read a novel more frightening and depressing; and yet, such are the originality, the suspense, the speed of writing and withering indignation that it is impossible to put the book down. The faults of Orwell as a writer — monotony, nagging, the lonely schoolboy shambling down the one dispiriting track — are transformed now he rises to a larger subject.

V. S. Pritchett. *New Statesman and Nation*, Vol. 37 (1949).

Brilliantly as he depicts and dramatizes the assault upon the individual will, Mr. Orwell is less successful when he tackles emotional relationships. The love affair which furnishes the fictional fillip of the book is shallow and unconvincing; one has the feeling that it bored the author as much as it does oneself. Mr. Orwell is very thoroughly an intellectual. He has, however, in *1984*, proved his ability to communicate his ideas in a manner calculated to rob many hours of sleep from every thinking reader.

David Burnham. *Commonweal*, Vol. 50 (1949).

1984 confirms its author in the special, honorable place he holds in our intellectual life . . . . It is a profound, terrifying and wholly fascinating book . . . . Orwell's theory of power is developed brilliantly, at considerable length. And the social system that it postulates is described with magnificent circumstantiality.

Lionel Trilling. *New Yorker*, Vol. 25 (1949).

George Orwell's novel escorts us so quietly, so directly, and so dramatically from our own day to the fate which may be ours in the future, that the experience is a blood-chilling one . . . . The story of official pursuit has all the suspense and melodrama of a super-detective novel, but instead of an exercise in criminal chase we are confronted with the grim pursuit that hangs over the head of every modern man.

William Soskin. *Saturday Review of Literature*, Vol. 32 (1949).

The book has many qualities as a thriller. The first half is as exciting as one could wish. But there is a flaw here. Just at the point where the excitement becomes excruciating and Winston and Julia launch out into their revolt against the party, Mr. Orwell maddeningly reminds us that all he's really interested in is the political implication of his story. He suspends the plot for thirty pages of Trotsky-Goldstein-Orwell analysis of contemporary political trends. And for the rest of the book he is concerned only with establishing the fact that no refinement of horror is beyond the Party's reach, not even that of making a man wholly love and believe in something which he knows is false and hateful.

Robert Kee. *Spectator*, Vol. 182 (1949).

It is pointless either to praise or blame Orwell for using the satirical method, since that is his natural medium. He is, in fact, the only first-rate satirist of our time. One can be glad he uses this method, for it probably gains him more readers for what he has to say than any other method would. But satire has one serious limitation: it is the least persuasive form of literature.

H. S. Tigner. *Christian Century*, Vol. 66 (1949).

Orwell's last work will undoubtedly rank as his greatest, though I suspect that *Animal Farm* will end by being the most popular, if only because it can be read as a fairy-tale by children. But *1984* has a far greater range of satirical force, and a grimness of power which could perhaps come only from the mind of a sick man. As literature, it has certain limitations. Satire, as Swift realised, becomes monotonous if carried too far in the same vein, and he therefore sent Gulliver to several different countries where human folly took on distinct guises. Though both writers have in common a savagery of indignation, the comparison of their work cannot be carried very far. Fundamental to Swift is a certain *disgust* of humanity and *despair* of life; fundamental to

Orwell is a *love* of humanity and a passionate desire to live in freedom. There is a difference of style, too, for though both practised a direct and unaffected narrative, Swift's is still playfully baroque – or, rather, baroquely playful. A more useful comparison is with Defoe – and this comparison holds good for the whole of Orwell's output. Defoe was the first writer to raise journalism to a literary art; Orwell perhaps the last. One could make direct comparisons between their writings if it would serve any purpose (between, say, *The Road to Wigan Pier* and the *Journal of the Plague Year*), but I prefer an indirect comparison between *1984* and *Robinson Crusoe.* The desert island is a long way from the totalitarian State; nevertheless, there is the same practicality in the construction of both books, and Winston Smith, 'his chin nuzzled into his breast in an effort to escape the vile wind', slipping 'quickly through the glass doors of Victory Mansions, though not quickly enough to prevent a swirl of gritty dust from entering along with him', is the same Little Man hero who, as Robinsoe Crusoe, being one day at Hull, 'went on board a ship bound for London ... without any consideration of circumstances or consequences, and in an ill hour, God knows.' Strictly speaking, *Robinson Crusoe* is neither a satire nor an Utopia, whereas *1984* is an Utopia in reverse – not an *Erewhon*, which is an Utopia upside-down. *Erewhon* is still written after the ameliorative pattern of *Utopia* itself: you may, paradoxically, be punished for being ill, but the ideal is health. In *1984* the pattern is malevolent; everything is for the worst in the worst of all possible worlds. But the pattern begins in the present – in our existing totalitarian States.

On page 157 there is a significant sentence which might be taken as the motif of the book: *By lack of understanding they remained sane.* The crime of Winston Smith, the hero of *1984*, was the use of a critical intelligence, his Socratic inability to stop asking questions. That 'ignorance is bliss' is no new discovery, but it has generally been assumed that understanding, which brings with it a sense of responsibility, an awareness of suffering and a tragic view of life, has compensations of a spiritual nature. It has been the object of modern tyrannies to deny man this sense of responsibility, and gradually to eliminate all feelings. The greatest enemies of the totalitarian State are not ideas (which can be dealt with dialectically) but aesthetic and erotic sensations. In the love of objective beauty, and in the love of an individual of the opposite sex, the most oppressed slave can escape to a free world. Religion is not so dangerous because it tends to be ideological and can be undermined by propaganda. But the sympathy of love, and the empathy of art — these feelings must be eradicated from the human breast if man's allegiance to Caesar (Big Brother) is to be complete. Orwell does not deal with the totalitarian hostility to art, but the dramatic quality which makes his satire so readable is due to his perception of the totalitarian hostility to love. " 'They can't get inside you,' she had said. But they could get inside you. 'What happens to you here is *for ever?*' O'Brien had said. That was a true word. There were things, your own acts, from which you could not recover. Something was killed in your breast: burnt out, cauterised out."

Herbert Read. *World Review*, No. 16 (1950).

Talking of *1984* and the future, I have been greatly interested recently to find that what I prophesied about 'Hypnopaedia' in *Brave New World* is now an accomplished fact. Pillow microphones attached to clock-controlled phonographs playing suitable recordings at regular intervals during the night are now being used quite extensively here by pediatricians who want to get rid of childish fears and bad habits, such as bed-wetting, or to help backward children acquire larger vocabularies, and by students who want to learn foreign languages in a quarter of the time ordinarily required for the job. (This device was largely employed by the U.S. Army in training men to acquire a working knowledge of colloquial Chinese or Japanese in a month or six weeks.) It looks very much as though the systematic brutality described in *1984* will seem to the really intelligent dictators of the future altogether too inefficient, messy and wasteful. Hypnopaedic methods can be used to make the rubber truncheon and the concentration camp unnecessary; and the ecstasy of satisfied power-lust can be obtained just as effectively from the spectacle of men and women conditioned into loving their servitude as by that of men and women driven by fear into unwilling obedience.

Aldous Huxley. *World Review*, No. 16 (1950).

The book cannot be understood, nor can it be properly valued, simply by resorting to the usual literary categories, for it posits a situation in which these categories are no longer significant. Everything has hardened into politics, the leviathan has swallowed the man. About such a world it is, strictly speaking, impossible to write a novel, if only because the human relationships taken for granted in the novel are here suppressed.

Irving Howe. *Politics and the Novel*, N.Y.: Harcourt, Brace and World (1957).

If Orwell had maintained a dramatic concreteness, *Nineteen Eighty-Four* would undoubtedly have been a more coherent work of art. Yet there were matters, such as the history of Oceania, the rationale behind the slave state, and the political significance of the debasement of language, which he felt impelled to include for ideological reasons and which could only be treated through expository devices like Goldstein's book, O'Brien's long monologues and the essay on newspeak. He obviously thought that it was more important to describe how certain social phenomena present in postwar civilization resulted in Oceania rather than to work in concrete and personal terms. If he sacrificed aesthetic integrity and cogency by failing to completely unify the political and human centers of the novel, he managed to clearly articulate a complex idea of what was occurring in society, where it could lead, and, lastly, an effective antidote for the disease.

David L. Kabul. *Outside the Whale: George Orwell's Art and Politics*, London: University of Notre Dame Press (1972).

The fantasy elements of *Nineteen Eighty-Four* thus reinforce only a part of Orwell's political purpose: that of exposing the audience to the nature of totalitarianism. The more hopeful side of his political faith, however, is left without imaginative support, and the book inexorably moves in a direction far from its original goal. This does not mean that the release of Orwell's imagination has destroyed his book, though it may have altered his preliminary intention beyond recognition. The expressive component of his fantasy world must be judged not by whether it serves his socialist commitment, nor by whether it violates the traditional assumptions of a genre, nor even by whether his obsessions are "morbid." Nor does the persuasiveness of such a work depend on how closely its vision corresponds to reality. The essential question is whether the writer's imagination expresses something absolutely idiosyncratic, or whether his extreme distortions are recognizable to many readers and in some sense acknowledged as their own. The extraordinary popularity of *Nineteen Eight-Four* — the fact that almost every serious reader knows the book — offers indisputable testimony that Orwell's obsession is shared. His vision may be selective and intense, but it is hardly unrecognizable.

Alex Zwerdling. *Orwell and the Left.* New Haven, Conn.: Yale University Press (1974).

The most common cliché of Orwell criticism is that *1984* (1949) is a 'nightmare vision' of the future. I believe, on the contrary, that it is a very concrete and naturalistic portrayal of the present and the past, and that its great originality results more from a realistic synthesis and rearrangement of familiar materials than from any prophetic or imaginary speculations. *1984* is not only a paradigm of the history of Europe for the previous twenty years, but also a culmination of all the characteristic beliefs and ideas expressed in Orwell's works from the Depression to the cold war. The origins of the novel can be found in Orwell's earliest books, and its major themes, precise symbols and specific passages can be traced very exactly throughout his writings. For example, Orwell characteristically expresses the poverty and isolation that oppresses the characters in his novels in terms of personal humiliation, so that Winston's sexual experience with his wife Katharine (who is frigid like Elizabeth in *Burmese Days* and Dorothy in *A Clergyman's Daughter*) is exactly like that of Gordon with Rosemary in *Keep the Aspidistra Flying*.

Orwell felt he had to frighten people into a painful recognition of the dangers that threatened their very existence.

Jeffrey Meyers. *A Reader's Guide to George Orwell.* London: Thames and Hudson (1975).

.That is the real warning and, to put it more strongly, the threat of Orwell's *1984*: it is the most thorough-going account in modern literature of a society altogether in the grip of fantasy. The fact that, in its manner of telling, it appears to be one man's fantasy, a single point of view, merely reinforces the effect. It is, notoriously, the unanimity of the society Orwell imagined that makes it so horrible: the story could in fact be described as the merging of a "single point of view" in collective fantasy. Again, we can call the fate of this singular man, Orwell's Winston Smith, a dream; but it is an evil dream which, by the end, everyone in the book shares, by implication the entire population of the world, and from which no one is ever going to wake up.

Christopher Small. *The Road to Miniluv: George Orwell, The State, and God*. London: Victor Gollancz Ltd. (1975).

A few [Polish writers] have become acquainted with Orwell's *1984*; because it is both difficult to obtain and dangerous to possess, it is known only to certain members of the Inner Party. Orwell fascinates them through his insight into details they know well, and through his use of Swiftian satire. Such a form of writing is forbidden by the New Faith because allegory, by nature manifold in meaning, would trespass beyond the prescriptions of socialist realism and the demands of the censor. Even those who know Orwell only by hearsay are amazed that a writer who never lived in Russia should have so keen a perception into its life. The fact that there are writers in the West who understand the functioning of the unusually constructed machine of which they themselves are a part astounds them and argues against the 'stupidity' of the West.

Czeslaw Milosz. *George Orwell: The Critical Heritage*. London: Routledge and Kegan Paul (1975).

Review Questions and Answers

Question 1.
Discuss the nature of characterization in *1984*.

Answer

1984 contains only two characters who are complete, multi-dimensional human beings. These are Winston Smith and, to a much lesser extent, Julia. The other characters in the book are either vaguely drawn or "types." The reason for this lack of real characters is, first of all, that the novel is politically satirical. The society Orwell depicts in his novel is such that individualized characters are rare. Most people in Oceania are rigidly conformed to a single mode by the pressures of the Party. Only rarely do individuals develop as individualists in Oceania. Thus, if would seem strange if Orwell, having presented such a repressive totalitarian society, had populated it with fully developed, many-dimensional characters. Another reason for the lack of individualized characters is that Winston Smith is an Everyman character, that is, his plight could be the plight of any reasonably intelligent and sensitive person, given similar circumstances. Since Smith represents every thinking man, it is not necessary for Orwell to have several well-defined and developed characters.

Question 2.
Discuss examples of Orwell's careful choice of names or physical characteristics for the main characters in *1984*.

Answer

Orwell obviously paid great attention to the names he chose for his characters and the physical attributes he gave them. The name "Winston Smith" was carefully chosen. It indicates both the universality and the uniqueness of the character. "Smith" is the most common English surname in the world, while "Winston," a much rarer common name, suggests Winston Churchill, who was perhaps the most well-known Englishman at the time of the novel's composition. Smith is intelligent and sensitive, but he differs from most modern protagonists in that his plight is one that is not uniquely his own. Any intelligent and sensitive person under the same conditions would react in the same way. That there are few intelligent and sensitive men in Oceania in 1984 does not show a lack of universality of the novel, but instead confirms the power of the Party. Orwell was not speaking to 1984 — he was speaking to his own post-World War II world, hoping to impress upon the Everyman of his time the importance of maintaining freedom and certain inalienable rights in the face of extreme pressures from whatever source they might come.

The name "Julia" was also carefully chosen. It immediately suggests Juliet, the Shakespearean character whose name has become inextricably connected with romantic love. Julia represents Woman, just as Winston Smith represents the intelligent Everyman. That we do not know her last name is significant, in that we are led not to think of her as an individual — not as *the* woman, but as *a* woman. In this regard, it is important to remember that Winston does not even learn her name until after she has appeared several times in the opening sections. As a matter of fact, the only main character for whom we have two names is Winston Smith.

The physical description of Big Brother is significant. The large, black mustache was obviously meant to represent Josef Stalin, the wartime leader of the Soviet Union who was responsible for several bloody purges within the Communist Party. However, it would be a mistake to infer from this resemblance between Big Brother and Stalin that *1984* is a satire directed at Communism or Stalinist Russia. Stalin was the epitome of a strong leader. He was later denounced for his ruthlessness and his development of a "cult of personality." It is in this light that the resemblance between Stalin and the leader of Ingsoc is significant. Big Brother is the supreme leader. Indeed, the primary reason for his creation by the Party is to satisfy the need for a single leader, with whom the people of Oceania can identify. He has been given a certain paternal aspect by the Party, which is, at the same time, threatening. In this, Big Brother also resembles Stalin.

"Emmanuel Goldstein" is also a significant name choice. The name is unmistakably Jewish. Orwell was not being anti-semitic in choosing a Jewish-sounding name. Goldstein is opposed to the system and is the symbol of opposition to Big Brother. If we accept the resemblance between Big Brother and Josef Stalin, then Goldstein is suggestive of Leon Trotsky, who was of the Hebrew faith. Trotsky was a rival of Stalin's for power in Russia after the death of Lenin, the leader of the Russian Revolution. Because of his opposition to Stalin, Trotsky soon fell into disgrace, fled the country and was finally assassinated in Mexico City. As in the relationship of Big Brother and Stalin, it would be a mistake to think of Emmanuel Goldstein as actually representing Leon Trotsky. The relationship between the two becomes significant only when we know that Trotsky became, within Communist circles, a symbol of opposition to the policies of Stalin. Thus, the relationship of the powerful and those who oppose them is introduced implicitly. Significantly, the Hebrew word "Emmanuel" means "messiah" or "savior." Since it appears that Goldstein is also a creation of the Party, he is actually a false prophet. This proves to be true, because he is used to lure the potential dissidents into the hands of the Party.

Question 3.
Do Winston's dreams reveal his character?

Answer
Writing *1984* when he did (1945-1949), Orwell was aware of Freudian dream interpretations. He quite possibly expected the dreams he included within his novel to be interpreted in terms of elementary Freudian psychology. Freudian psychology holds that repressed feelings make themselves known through dreams. It is in this light that Winston's character is further revealed through his dreams. From his dreams, we learn that Winston desires Julia. This dreaming about Julia and the beautiful Golden Country reveals his repressed sexual desire and aspiration for freedom and beauty. From his dreams, we also learn that Winston treated his mother and sister very badly. This is an expression of a guilt feeling, which may go a long way toward explaining why Winston trusted O'Brien, even though he later admits that he knew all long that O'Brien was not what he seemed. Perhaps Winston, as many people with guilt complexes do, desired punishment for his obnoxious treatment of his mother and starving sister. From one of his dreams, Winston wakes with the name "Shakespeare" on his lips. This is quite possibly illustrative of Winston's repressed resentment against the Party for destroying literature and the English language and replacing it with Newspeak. These dreams provide the reader with important hints concerning the character of Winston Smith.

Question 4.
Discuss the differences between the characters of Winston and Julia.

Answer
The chief difference in the characters of Winston and Julia is illustrated in the different natures of their rebellion against the Party. Winston's rebellion is emotional and intellectual; for the most part, while Julia's is primarily physical. She is not interested in questions of ideology or politics. Her main motivating force is her search for physical pleasure. Winston is the last in a long line of her lovers. This is not to say, however, that her love for Winston is not sincere. However, her love is almost completely on a physical level. Thus it is not surprising when we learn indirectly that she betrays her lover almost immediately when placed under torture, as she had predicted she would. Intellectually, Julia is limited. Also, it is significant that she is much less interested in human suffering than is Winston.

Winston's revolt, on the other hand, is intellectual, emotional and physical. Winston is gifted with an insatiable curiosity. From the beginning of the book, we see Winston groping toward an awareness of himself and his world. This search for answers is one of the main motivating forces in Winston's character. The Party is forced to spend much more time and effort in breaking down his resistance than it expends on Julia, because Winston is more intelligent than Julia, and his rebellion is on a deeper plane than hers.

Winston is a complex character. Julia, while less complex than Winston, is not a two-dimensional or "flat" character — she comes very much alive in the novel. We cannot forget that Winston's revolt is also partly physical. Orwell, in *1984* and in other works, draws a definite parallel between sexual freedom and political freedom. Julia's physical desire is also in part a desire for political freedom since, in Oceanic society, sexual abandonment conflicts with the aims of the Party. It is enough to say that neither character is heroic, but their interests and reasons for disenchantment with the Party differ. Julia is concerned with the physical and the practical. Winston is also concerned with the physical, but more profoundly with things of the spirit and the intellect. He is concerned with his and Julia's safety, but he is also interested in more abstract values. He is in search of a stable reality in a society in which reality does not remain stable.

Question 5.
Discuss the function of O'Brien.

Answer
O'Brien's character does not really develop through the novel. We learn that his chief motivating force is the need for power, just as the Party's reason for being is power. In a very real way, O'Brien symbolizes the Party and abstract evil as much as Big Brother does. In religious terminology, Big Brother is the god of an evil-worshipping world and O'Brien is His high priest. Furthermore, since Big Brother does not really exist, the oligarchy (elite) that rules Oceania is itself the God. O'Brien's function as a member of this elite is to "save" Winston. His relationship with Winston Smith is complex. He is both teacher and torturer and is both patient and ruthless. The bizarre and elaborate measures, which the Party takes to ensure the capture and rehabilitation of Winston, are a testament to the intelligence of O'Brien, and to the abstract value he sees in Winston as a challenge to the power of the Party.

Question 6.
Describe the plot structure of the novel and its functions.

Answer
The plot structure of *1984* is logical and, by and large, chronological. The only departures from a chronological sequence are the clearly defined dreams and flashbacks. We can say that *1984* is a record of the decline, fall and salvation of an individual. But, of course, the novel is much more than that. The plot also reveals something about the operations of a totalitarian government and the motives behind those operations. Winston Smith is an individual, but he is also Everyman, or at least every intelligent man.

The functions of the plot structure are numerous. First of all, the chronological sequence enables Orwell to tell a consistently interesting and logically developed story. The plot, concerning as it does an extraordinary individual who at the same time is representative of all intelligent and sensitive men, allows

Orwell to relate a particularized story that is also universal. The development of the plot in terms of both the fall and final salvation of Winston, and also the political structure and ultimate triumph of the Party, permits Orwell to integrate into one work both human experience and sociological theory. The plot structure is such that Orwell is able to combine the techniques of both the novelist and the dramatist. That is to say, the novel is divided into a series of interdependent but individual scenes, much as is a play, but they are all told from the most characteristic position of the novelist, the third person point of view.

One important basis of the plot is the Party's idea of the past. Just as Winston Smith is required in his job to constantly make the past conform to the present, so he himself must be "revised" to conform with the Party's idea of what a good citizen should be. As O'Brien tells him, he will exist or cease to exist at the pleasure of the Party. It seems certain that Winston will eventually become an "unperson," one who has never existed at all. This probability, of which the reader is convinced, indicates the absolute power of a totalitarian government.

On the basis of this idea, the plot could be said to move in the manner of overlapping curves, and it peaks at three points, each of which is a climax, the second one being the major climax of the story: when Winston and Julia make love for the first time; when they are arrested; and when Winston capitulates in Room 101. It is a relatively simple, certainly straightforward plot. Since Winston's fate is apparent almost from the first page of the novel, the suspense it creates comes from the reader's unwillingness to believe that the inevitable will actually happen.

Question 7.
Outline the nature of daily life in the novel.

Answer
The physical facts which Orwell devised for the society of Oceania are projections of the world as he saw it in the 1940s. Victory Mansions, where Winston Smith lives, is a London tenement almost ready to collapse; Victory Gin is cheap liquor universally consumed; the uniform worn by Party members, whether Inner or Outer, is a coverall like that worn by mechanics; the enormous buildings housing the four ministries

are functionally designed by an architect under orders to get as many rooms into one structure as possible; and so forth.

In the lives of Winston and Julia, as well as Parsons, Syme, Tillotson and the others, Oceania is a society whose aim is the greatest good for the smallest number. The tone of daily life, epitomized in the twenty-four-hour-a-day fabrications on the telescreen, is set by the ruling class so that everyone is forever in need of cigarettes, chocolate, shoes, ordinary conversational pleasantries, companionship, sexual satisfaction and ideas. Winston, like all others, is expected to do his job efficiently and receive no reward but the opportunity to live austerely for the greater good and self-perpetuation of the Inner Party. The highest reward is the chance to hate the enemy — whomever the Party designates at the moment — for two minutes, regularly and with hysterical conviction.

What Winston does not have is freedom. This is what Orwell saw disappearing, in various ways, in his own time, along with decency, common humanity and honesty. These values are conspicuously absent in the society depicted in the novel.

Question 8.
Outline the major divisions of *1984*.

Answer
1984 is divided into three parts. The first part contains action occurring over a period of several months. This initial division provides the exposition, that is, the introduction of the major characters and a description of the society in which they live. The major function of this first part is to present Winston Smith's growing awareness of himself as an individual and of the horrors of the totalitarian world in which he exists.

Part II begins with Winston's discovery of Julia and their growing love. The section ends with their betrayal to the Thought Police. This part illustrates the actual rebellion.

The third division is concerned with Winston's treatment and conversion in the Ministry of Love. This short, horror-filled section is the most disheartening part of the novel. All hope for any alternative has disappeared. Big Brother and the Party have triumphed. Winston, at the end of the novel, is a mere shell of a man.

Question 9.
Discuss the function of Part I.

Answer
The function of Part I is to introduce most of the principal characters (Julia, Winston, O'Brien) and to illustrate the structure of society in 1984.

Part I deals with the decline of Winston's relationship with his society. It shows his growing awareness that the Party is completely immoral and corrupt. For the reader, this section illustrates the Party's dehumanizing influence on the people of Oceania, its use of terror and intimidation, its systematic falsification of history and reality (even to the point that dreams seem more real than states of consciousness) and its pervasive presence in all aspects of life so that nothing is personal or private. The first part of the novel also introduces Julia and O'Brien, and Winston's growing consciousness of them, his feeling that they are somehow tied up inextricably with himself. Part I is similar to the first act of a drama. The reader has met the characters (though he does not know very much about two of them) and knows something about the scene in which the action takes place. Orwell has built up a feeling of suspense as the first part ends.

Question 10.
Discuss the function of Part II.

Answer
Part II chronicles the fall of Winston Smith. He began his revolt at the very beginning of the novel by starting his diary, but the break with the Party reaches its most crucial point in this second part. His relationship with Julia adds another dimension to the novel. Winston's revolt is primarily emotional and intellectual. Julia's revolt is almost purely physical. In this part, Orwell connects political and sexual freedom. The relationship of Winston and O'Brien suggests that the Party has spent much time on Winston Smith, going to such lengths as to create the bizarre and complicated trap that finally ensnares Winston and Julia. Part III, which follows, explains why the Party has taken such elaborate measures. Goldstein's treatise, *The Theory and Practice of Oligarchal Collectivism*, is important in that it reveals

the historical background of Oceanic society, describes the structures within the society and explains the political theory on which that society is based. Throughout Part II there is a growing sense of fatality. But our curiosity is not satisfied; we wonder what will happen. We are still not certain as to the motives of the Party. We want to know more about O'Brien and Goldstein, and we want to know whether Winston will be able to maintain his individuality, at least within himself, and whether Julia can maintain her free nature. Part II, however, ends on a note of despair, but that ending was not unexpected. Part III begins the final and most horrifying section of *1984*.

Question 11.
What is the function of Part III?

Answer
Part III is concerned with the Party's "salvation" of Winston Smith. The Party's methods of salvation consist of brainwashing and torture. It is necessary that Winston understand exactly what is happening to him before he can be "saved." In Part III, we witness a strange relationship develop between Smith and his torturer O'Brien. Part III contains the most explanatory scenes of the novel. Orwell has carefully prepared us for this section by introducing key elements into the previous sections and posing questions about the motives of the Party. The function of this third section is that of resolution. The section resolves the questions raised by the earlier sections and ends with the inevitable, though unpleasant, victory of Big Brother and the Party.

Question 12.
Can the novel be interpreted merely as a satire on communism?

Answer
In part, yes, but *1984* is much too universal a novel to be merely a satire on communism. Orwell does employ some satirical references to communist figures and policies. Big Brother and Emmanuel Goldstein are intentionally suggestive of Josef Stalin and Leon Trotsky, but in this novel, Orwell is simply using Stalin as a symbol of strong, ruthless leadership and Trotsky as a symbol of scapegoatish opposition in order to give

greater credibility and depth to his characters. The Party's use of Three-Year Plans is similar in terminology to the Russian series of Five-Year Plans. In only one instance is there serious satire directed primarily at the communists. In that instance, Orwell points out that although everything done by the Party in Oceania is done in the name of English Socialism (Ingsoc), the Party denies every principle of the socialist movement. As a socialist himself, Orwell felt that Soviet communism was a falsification of true socialism. But, of course, even this criticism by Orwell, that the Party says one thing and does another, is not directed solely at Russia — Orwell felt the West was equally guilty of hypocrisy. He despised the managerial, bureaucratic and industrial society of England and the United States. He saw in it the same seeds of doublethink and official hypocrisy that come to full bloom in Oceanic society.

The oligarchical collectivist society of Oceania did not come about as a result of communist revolution. It is reported that, at the end of World War II, Orwell mistakenly feared that Stalin, Churchill and Roosevelt (wartime leaders of the three strongest victorious powers, the Soviet Union, Britain and the United States) were plotting the permanent division of the world. Thus, it is unlikely that Orwell intended *1984* as a satire against communism alone. Communism was only one of the dangerous trends in his society that Orwell feared and attacked in the novel. He saw the abuse of power as a worrisome trend in *all* states, not just the communist ones.

Question 13.
How does Orwell connect the themes of political and sexual freedom in *1984*?

Answer
The Party in *1984* has declared war on sexual freedom. Like all totalitarian regimes, Ingsoc fears sex because it is a manifestation of the traditional concepts of love, marriage and family. Love is dangerous to the Party because it demands loyalty to an individual other than Big Brother. The sexual activity that does take place is sordid and degrading, completely divorced from romantic love.

The Party is not interested in merely discouraging sexual activity. Its purposes are more devious than that. The Party is interested in diverting the sexual drive into appropriate political action. The Party capitalizes on the hysteria and anxiety created by sexual starvation. On the other hand, it also uses sexual excess as a narcotic for the proles. The sexual policy of the Party, then, is ambivalent. The Party's encouragement of sexual excess has as its purpose the distraction of the proles. But, for the supposed elite, the Outer Party members, the Party encourages abstinence. The Party then attempts to translate the anxiety and hysteria caused by sexual repression into party loyalty and fanaticism.

Thus, the connection between sexual and political freedom stems from the circumstances of society in the year 1984. Sexual freedom is a political offence for Outer Party members. The connection between the two freedoms in the novel is strengthened, however, by the natures of the two leading characters. Winston and Julia's sexual expression is the only positive action they can take against a corrupt, thoroughly immoral society. As such, it gains in moral value when viewed as a protest against the ultimate evil of Ingsoc. Orwell celebrates a healthy sexuality. His greatest fear, in his last years, was that the sexual drive might be controlled and directed toward political ends by unscrupulous dictators, as it is in *1984*.

Question 14.
Why does the Party spend so much time and effort on one individual like Winston Smith?

Answer
Winston Smith has somehow managed to retain a curiosity about what the past was really like. For some reason, he has been able to withstand the psychological bombardment of the Party. He has kept within him a spirit of humanity and a feeling for aesthetics. This is what makes him unique. His thoughtcrime, though it is petty as an actual threat to the security of the Party, is an example of the Party's failure to perfect its techniques of indoctrination.

For men like O'Brien, who have as their goal the exercise of complete power, this failure is unbearable. The Party cannot fail. To make a mistake is to be weak. The Party, therefore, must be minutely conscious of all thoughtcrime and must be perfectly thorough in correcting all deviation from their desired patterns of thought.

The Party spends great time and effort on Winston Smith because he is unique — he is an intelligent, sensitive individual in a society in which "ignorance is strength." Because of the nature of the ruling class, whose only object is power, Winston becomes a major test of the Party's power.

Question 15.

Is there a parallel between government and religion in *1984*?

Answer

In designing the governmental structure of Oceania, Orwell clearly intended the government to reflect distinctly religious overtones. The various aspects of the government are patterned after Christian concepts and symbols, with their original meanings twisted to their opposites. The most evident of these symbols is the number, three. Just as the significance of that number is obvious in the Christian concept of the Trinity, so is the Party's use of the number significant in its three slogans. In Christian terms, the Church is divided into three parts or stages: the Church Militant, the Church Expectant and the Church Triumphant. Oceanic society is divided into three classes: the Inner Party, the Outer Party and the proles. Life after death, according to traditional Christian dogma, may be divided into three areas: Heaven, Purgatory and Hell. The world in 1984 is divided into three states: Oceania, Eurasia and Eastasia. Other parallel uses of the number three could be discovered, but the above are enough to indicate that Orwell uses the number intentionally.

It is significant, too, that the important divisions of the government — the Ministry of Truth, the Ministry of Love, the Ministry of Peace and the Ministry of Plenty — are named for Christian ideals. It should not be overlooked that the novel is divided into three parts and follows, ironically, the Christian pattern of original sin, fall from grace and ultimate redemption. Christianity and Ingsoc both require emotional rather than intellectual responses. Christ requires sinners to "come as little children;" Big Brother, in the novel, requires fanatical loyalty. In Oceania, crimes are considered sins against the Party; instead of punishing the sinner, the Party "saves" him. A further parallel is evident in the structure of Oceanic society and in that of the

Christian hierarchy. That is, the small governing class of the church; the priest class, and the large class of laymen. In addition, the timelessness of the Party is suggestive of the infinite nature of God. This parallel is strengthened by the semi-mystical nature of Big Brother as he is presented in the novel. He is physically absent yet always present.

Special attention should be paid to the correspondence of the most important Christian figures and concepts with the most important Oceanic personages and devices. Big Brother, as noted in the prvious paragraph, is the God figure. It is in his name that the work of the Party is done. Just as the Church embodies the spirit of God and does His worldly work, the Party does the will of Big Brother. Both supreme beings are known by familial names — one as "father," the other as "brother." Both are physically absent.

If Big Brother is the God figure of Oceania, then O'Brien is the Christ or high-priest figure. He is described as doctor, teacher and priest, three roles attributed to Christ. It is he who "saves" Winston and other sinners in a demonic and soul-destroying way. The Party, the spirit of Ingsoc, corresponds to the third member of the Christian Trinity, the Holy Ghost.

Emmanuel Goldstein is, in the system of parallels, the Satan equivalent. He is the fallen angel transformed into the evil enemy of Big Brother. His first name is a Hebrew word for "messiah," thus indicating the reverse religion of Oceania in which Satan is also the "messiah." Winston and Julia are the Oceanic Adam and Eve. The telescreen, doublethink and crimestop serve in place of the Christian conscience, imposed from outside rather than rising from within.

The most important parallels between Oceanic government and the Christian religion are the following: the familiar Christian process by which sinful man is freed from guilt consists of confession, repentance and absolution; the Party's three stages of "reintegration" are learning, understanding and acceptance. These steps represent, in order, the intellectual response, the emotional reaction and the total surrender. Both the Christian religion and the Party give promise of certain kinds of immortality. Christianity promises an afterlife. The Party promises a mystical union of godliness and the individual. That is, the individual, through enforced loyalty and love toward Big Brother, loses his individuality by absorption into the eternal Party.

Question 16.
List several important symbols in the novel.

Answer
Orwell's use of symbolism is both natural and effective. Some symbols express Winston's hope for a better life: the dream of the Golden Country and the glass paperweight. Others show his nostalgia for the past: the print on the wall of the room and the nursery rhyme. Still others embody his fears: rats and Room 101. Many of them help to measure the changes that occur to him. For instance, the paperweight, at first representing his wish for a life apart from the impersonal world of Oceania, is smashed by the Thought Police when he and Julia are arrested. The chance for that life apart is also destroyed.

Question 17.
Is Orwell's style appropriate to the subject matter of *1984*?

Answer
In *1984* the style is very well suited to the subject matter. As stated previously, Orwell's purpose in writing the novel was to make his fellow men aware of the possible results of the barbaric trends he perceived in his own society. He wanted to paint a picture of a society so terrifying and corrupt, yet logical and within the realm of possibility, that others would become aware of the dangers inherent in militarism, brutality, oppression and conformity. This he succeeds in doing in *1984*. He portrays a drab, colorless society with a lucidity and precision that is remarkable for its sharpness. While it is true that a book about dull people doesn't have to be dull, Orwell obviously intended his novel about a terrifying system of government to *be* terrifying. Through his careful attention to detail and his meticulous search for exactness, Orwell creates an anti-utopia so believable that most readers are shocked into thought about their own society, and its resemblances to the society Orwell depicts so graphically.

While the novel has certain of the characteristics of Orwell's journalistic style, it is a great deal more than mere reporting. Orwell has the ability to write in commonplace prose which, at its best, is accurate and easily understandable. He is particularly good at two things: getting the exact detail to describe daily life, for instance, the way the tobacco in Victory Cigarettes is loosely packed; and embodying political ideas in such a way as to reveal their truth or falsity, as, for example, in the slogans and rules of the Party. Both are used to good effect in the novel and are highly suited to the subject.

Question 18.
Discuss the point of view of the novel.

Answer
1984 is told from the third person point of view by a neutral, omniscient narrator. That is, the narrator is not himself involved in the action of the story and is in a position to know the whole story. He can, for instance, comment on the thoughts of Winston even when they are not expressed in dialogue. Orwell's is a "neutral" narrator in that he does not explicitly make moral judgments. That is not to state that Orwell himself is neutral; obviously, he is not neutral at all. The choice of episodes and the sympathetic treatment of the character, Winston, point to the moral indignation with which Orwell viewed his fictional society. But, Orwell as narrator makes his disapproval felt only indirectly. He does not, for example, say in so many words, "dear reader, this is an evil society." What he does do is to present episodes which make it obvious to the reader that the society of Oceania is evil and corrupt. He creates a character with which readers can sympathize and empathize and then subjects him to the oppression of a completely evil society. Through this method, Orwell is able to make significant moral judgments implicitly; he does not have to preach. Through the reader's sympathy with Winston, the pain and the injustice of his final conversion are brought home strongly and effectively.

It is true that, in a novel of this kind, characters are present in part to embody an idea. But, the way in which Winston and the others are shown to represent certain ideas is believable. Winston's revolt against conformity, for instance, is as imperfect and as inept as that of any human being would be.

The most important use of point of view, surely, is the way in which it dramatizes Winston as "the last man" in a society dedicated to forcing the individual to disappear into the image of Big Brother.

Bibliography

Alver, Leonard. "The Relevance of George Orwell," *English Literature and Language Studies*, Vol. 8 (1971).

Atkins, John. *George Orwell: A Literary Study*. London: Calder and Boyars (new edition, orig. 1955), 1971.

Barr, Alan. "The Paradise Behind *1984*," *English Miscellany*, Vol. 19 (1968).

Beauchamp, Gorman L. "Future Words: Language and the Dystopian Novel," *Style*, Vol. 8 (1974).

Brander, Laurence. *George Orwell*. N.Y.: Longmans, Green and Co., 1954.

Connors, James. " 'Do it to Julia': Thoughts on Orwell's *1984*," *Modern Fiction Studies*, Vol. 16 (1970).

_____. "Zamyatin's *We* and the Genesis of *1984*," *Modern Fiction Studies*, Vol. 21 (1975).

Crowcroft, Peter. "Politics and Writing: The Orwell Analysis," *New Republic*, No. 132 (3 Jan. '55).

Dooley, D. J. "The Freudian Critics of *1984*," *Triumph*, Vol. 1 (1974).

Elsbree, Langdon. "The Structured Nightmare of *1984*," *Twentieth Century*, Vol. 5 (1959).

Ferguson, Alfred R. "Newspeak, the First Edition: Tyranny and the Decay of Language," *Michigan Quarterly Review*, Vol. 14 (1975).

Gross, Miriam, ed. *The World of George Orwell*. N.Y.: Simon and Schuster, 1971.

Gulbin, Suzanne. "Parallels and Contrasts in *Lord of the Flies* and *1984*," *English Journal*, Vol. 55 (1966).

Harris, Harold J. "Orwell's Essays and *1984*," *Twentieth Century*, Vol. 4 (1959).

Hollis, Cristopher. *A Study of George Orwell: The Man and his Works*. Chicago: Henry Regnery Co., 1956.

Hopkinson, Tom. *George Orwell*. London: Longmans, Green. 1962 (2nd edition).

Howe, Irving, ed. *Orwell's 1984: Text, Sources, Criticism*. N.Y.: Harcourt, Brace, and World, 1963.

Hynes, Samuel, comp. *Twentieth-Century Interpretations of 1984: A Collection of Critical Essays*. Englewood Cliffs, N.J.: Prentice-Hall, 1971.

Kegal, Charles. "*1984*: A Century of Ingsoc," *Notes and Queries*, No. 208 (April 1963).

Lee, Robert A. *Orwell's Fiction*. Notre Dame, Ind.: University of Notre Dame Press, 1969.

Meyers, Jeffrey. *A Reader's Guide to George Orwell*. Totawa, N.J.: Littlefield and Adams, 1977.

_____. *George Orwell: An Annotated Bibliography of Criticism*. N.Y.: Garland, 1977.

_____. ed. *George Orwell: The Critical Heritage*. London: Routledge and Kegan Paul, 1975.

_____. "The Evolution of *1984*," *English Miscellany*, Vol. 23 (1972).

Oxley, B. T. *George Orwell*. London: Evans Bros., 1967.

Quennell, Peter and others. "*1984* Revisited: Reflections on Orwell's Predictions," *Daily Telegraph Magazine* (London), (20 September 1974).

Ranald, Ralph A. "George Orwell and the Mad World: The Anti-Universe of *1984*," *South Atlantic Quarterly*, Vol. 66 (1967).

Rankin, David. "Orwell's Intention in *1984*," *English Language Notes*, Vol. 12 (1975).

Rees, Sir Richard. *George Orwell: Fugitive from the Camp of Victory*. Carbondale, Ill.: Southern Illinois University Press, 1962.

Roazen, Paul. "Orwell, Freud, and *1984*," *Virginia Quarterly Review*, Vol. 54 (1978).

Slater, Joseph. "The Fictional Values of *1984*," *Essays in Literary History*, Vol. 16 (1961).

Small, Cristopher. *The Road to Miniluv: George Orwell, the State, and God*. Pittsburgh: The University of Pittsburgh Press, 1976.

Smith, Marcus. "The Wall of Blackness: A Psychological Approach to *1984*," *Modern Fiction Studies*, Vol. 14 (1968).

Steinhoff, William, *George Orwell and the Origins of 1984*. Ann Arbor, Mich.: University of Michigan Press, 1975.

_____. *The Road to 1984*. London: Weidenfeld, 1975.

Thomas, Edward M. *Orwell*. London: Oliver and Boyd, 1965.

Trilling, Lionel. "George Orwell and the Politics of Truth," in *The Opposing Self*. N.Y.: Viking Press, 1955.

Vorhees, Richard J. *The Paradox of George Orwell*. Lafayette, Ind.: Purdue University Press, 1961.

Warburg, Fredric. *Animal Farm and 1984: All Authors are Equal*. London, 1973.

97

Williams, Raymond, comp. *George Orwell: A Collection of Critical Essays*. Englewood Cliffs, N.J.: Prentice-Hall, 1974.
_____. *Orwell*. N.Y.: Viking Press, 1971.
Woodcock, George. *The Crystal Spirit: A Study of George Orwell*. London: Jonathan Cape, 1967.
Zamyatin, Eugene. *We*. N.Y.: E. P. Dutton and Co., Inc., 1959. (in English translation).
Zwerdling, Alex. *Orwell and the Left*. New Haven, Conn.: Yale University Press, 1974.

NOTES

NOTES

NOTES

NOTES

NOTES

NOTES

Don't forget to match that tough textbook with helpful
COLES NOTES

Shakespeare
Antony and Cleopatra
Antony and Cleopatra—Ques. and Ans.
As You Like It
Coriolanus
Hamlet
Hamlet in Everyday English
Hamlet—Ques. and Ans.
Julius Caesar
Julius Caesar in Everyday English
Julius Caesar—Ques. and Ans.
King Henry IV—Part 1
King Henry IV—Part 1
   —Ques. and Ans.
King Henry V
King Lear
King Lear in Everyday English
King Lear—Ques. and Ans.
Macbeth
Macbeth in Everyday English
Macbeth—Ques. and Ans.
Measure for Measure
Merchant of Venice
Merchant of Venice in Everyday English
Merchant of Venice—Ques. and Ans.
Midsummer Night's Dream
Midsummer Night's Dream in
   Everyday English
Midsummer Night's Dream—
   Ques. and Ans.
Much Ado About Nothing
Othello
Othello—Ques. and Ans.
Richard II
Richard III
Romeo and Juliet
Romeo and Juliet in Everyday English
Romeo and Juliet—Ques. and Ans.
Taming of the Shrew
Tempest
Twelfth Night
Winter's Tale

**Shakespeare Total
Study Editions**
Hamlet
Julius Caesar
King Henry IV—Part 1
King Lear
Macbeth
Measure for Measure
Merchant of Venice
Othello
Romeo and Juliet

Taming of the Shrew
Tempest
Twelfth Night

Reference
Dictionary of Literary Terms
Effective Term Papers and Reports
English Grammar Simplified
Handbook of English Grammar
   and Composition
How to Write Good Essays
   and Critical Reviews
Secrets of Studying English

The Canterbury Tales
Canterbury Tales
Prologue to the Canterbury Tales T.S.E.
Prologue to the Canterbury Tales

French
French Grammar—Ques. and Ans.
French Grammar Simplified
French Verbs Fully Conjugated
French Verbs Simplified

German
German Grammar—Ques. and Ans.
German Grammar Simplified

History
History of Canada
History of the United States

Mathematics
Elementary Algebra Notes
Secondary Sch. Maths 1
Secondary Sch. Maths 4
Senior Algebra Notes

Chemistry
Elementary Chemistry Notes—Revised
How to Solve Chemistry Problems
Introduction to Chemistry
Senior Chemistry Notes—Revised

Physics
Elementary Physics Notes
How to Solve Physics Problems
Senior Physics Notes

Biology
Biology Notes

Philosophy
Philosophy—Ques. and Ans.

Literature/Poetry
Adventures of Huckleberry Finn
Adventures of Tom Sawyer
All Quiet on the Western Front
Animal Farm
Bleak House
Brave New World/
   Brave New World Revisited
Catch 22
Catcher in the Rye, Nine Stories
Chrysalids, Day of the Triffids
Crime and Punishment
Crucible
Cry the Beloved Country
Death of a Salesman
Diviners
Doctor Faustus
Duddy Kravitz and Other Works
Edible Woman
Emma
Fahrenheit 451
Far From the Madding Crowd
Farewell to Arms
Fifth Business
For Whom the Bell Tolls
Frost's Poetry Notes
Glass Menagerie
Grapes of Wrath
Great Expectations
Great Gatsby
Gulliver's Travels
Hard Times
Heart of Darkness
Ibsen's Works
Iliad
Jane Fyre
Joseph Andrews
Keats' Poetry Notes
King Oedipus, Oedipus at Colonus,
   Antigone
Le Morte D'Arthur
Lord of the Flies
Lord of the Rings, Hobbit
Madame Bovary
Man for All Seasons
Mansfield Park
Mayor of Casterbridge
Mill on the Floss
Mrs. Dalloway, To the Lighthouse
Murder in the Cathedral
   & Selected Poems

1984
Odyssey
Of Mice and Men
Old Man and the Sea
Oliver Twist
One Flew Over the Cuckoo's Nest
Paradise Lost
Passage to India
Pearl
Persuasion
Pickwick Papers
Pilgrim's Progress

Portrait of the Artist as a Young Man
Power and the Glory
Pride and Prejudice
Prince-Machiavelli
Pygmalion
Rape of the Lock
Saint Joan
Scarlet Letter
Separate Peace
Sons and Lovers
Stone Angel and Other Works
Stranger, Plague
Streetcar Named Desire
Such is My Beloved, More Joy in Heaven
Sun Also Rises, Snows of Kilimanjaro

Surfacing
Tale of Two Cities
Tess of the D'Ubervilles
To Kill a Mockingbird
Tom Jones
Two Solitudes
Ulysses
Vanity Fair
Waiting for Godot
War and Peace
Who Has Seen the Wind
Wordsworth's Poetry Notes
Works of John Donne
Wuthering Heights
Yeats' Poetry Notes